touching the holy

Ordinariness, Self-Esteem, and Friendship

SPIRITUAL GROWTH AND PROFESSIONAL DEVELOPMENT BOOKS BY ROBERT J. WICKS

• •

Streams of Contentment
Prayerfulness
Crossing the Desert
Overcoming Secondary Stress in Medical and Nursing Practice
Riding the Dragon
Snow Falling on Snow
Simple Changes
Everyday Simplicity
Sharing Wisdom
Living a Gentle, Passionate Life
After 50: Embracing Your Own Wisdom Years
Circle of Friends (with Robert Hamma)
Seeds of Sensitivity
Living Simply in an Anxious World
Availability

touching the holy

Ordinariness, Self-Esteem, and Friendship

Robert J. Wicks

SORIN BOOKS Notre Dame, Indiana

All rights reserved. No part of this book may be used or reproduced in any manner whatsoever, except in the case of reprints in the context of reviews, without written permission from Sorin Books®, P.O. Box 428, Notre Dame, IN 46556-0428.

www.sorinbooks.com

ISBN-10 1-933495-02-2   ISBN-13 978-1-933495-02-6

Cover and text design by John Carson

Printed and bound in the United States of America.

CIP data is available from the Library of Congress.

green press
INITIATIVE

For my daughter Michaela

Contents

Introduction

Surprisingly, the real, refreshing, and mysterious challenge of the spiritual life is not primarily to give love, but to *receive* it. For when our hearts are alive with love, we can, and do, spontaneously share with a sense of *mitzvah* (giving and expecting nothing in return)! As Pope John XXIII said many years ago: "Whoever has a heart full of love, always has something to share." And so, with a healthy sense of self-love, the call from God to love others as we love ourselves is transformed from an exterior command into a powerful interior attitude of hope that can lead to true compassion, sound friendship, and effective social action.

However, our own sometimes shaky self-esteem, neediness, and failure to believe that we are really unique in the eyes of God often prevent us from loving and nurturing the presence of God in ourselves. This, in turn, makes it difficult to reach out to others. We're paralyzed by a lack of self-confidence and the anxiety that inordinate fear produces. Consequently, the deep, negative, doubtful feelings we have about ourselves must be dissolved by sowing new corrective healing seeds in the unconscious and by letting go of the obvious and subtle addictions that have entangled and entrapped us. We need to appreciate anew the beauty of *ordinariness*: God loves and has already gifted us in so many ways.

In doing this, as many spiritual guides have shown, we will be better able to develop a more solid self-esteem based on trust in God. We will also stop the unnecessary drain of energy that is so frequently wasted in psychological self-defense and running to other images of self. We will not avoid the challenges before us because of a lack of personal strength. Rather, we will be in a good position to receive the grace to see and seek new channels of life for ourselves as well as for those who suffer and especially need to share in a sense of God's peace at this point in their lives. In other words: we will be in a situation that draws us to spend less time in thinking about "the spiritual life" and more time actually living it.

To provide support for this, in the following pages will explore ordinariness, true self-esteem, and the four types of friends necessary for the spiritual journey. These themes are closely interrelated, for in each of them we can see how we can touch the holy in a profound way, every day.

Robert J. Wicks
Loyola College, Maryland
August 2006

Part One

ORDINARINESS

One

EMBRACING ORDINARINESS

*T*rue ordinariness is tangible holiness. We can sense this particularly when we are with persons who have the courage and trust in God to "simply be themselves."

Jim Fenhagen, the Dean of General Theological Seminary, relates the story of a seminarian who was sitting near him during an address by Archbishop Desmond Tutu. After the talk was over, the student turned to Dean Fenhagen and said: "Today I met a holy man." When he asked the student to elaborate, he replied that in Tutu's presence he was able to experience Christ in his own life.[1]

I think all of us have experienced this with certain people. I remember visiting someone who was so real, undefensive, accepting, and self-aware that during the visit I felt no stress or anxiety at all. I could be myself; it was enough. I even had the strange sensation after I left him that I had not aged while in his presence! After all, how could I? There was no pressure when I was with him.

Truly ordinary people have a way of awakening us to recognize our deep-seated pride and biases. This is revealed in a striking way in Robert Coles' account of an encounter with Dorothy Day, the co-founder along with Peter Maurin of the Catholic Worker Movement:

> It was on (an) afternoon, almost thirty-five years ago, that I first met Dorothy Day. She was sitting at a table, talking with a woman who was, I quickly realized, quite drunk, yet determined to carry on a conversation. The woman . . . had a large purple-red birthmark along the right side of her forehead. She kept touching it as she uttered one exclamatory remark after another, none of which seemed to get the slightest rise from the person sitting opposite her.
>
> I found myself increasingly confused by what seemed to be an interminable, essentially absurd exchange taking place between the two middle-aged women. When would it end—the alcoholic ranting and the silent nodding, occasionally

interrupted by a brief question, which only served, maddeningly, to wind up the already overtalkative one rather than wind her down? Finally silence fell upon the room. Dorothy Day asked the woman if she would mind an interruption. She got up and came over to me. She said, "Are you waiting to talk with one of us?"

One of us: with those three words she had cut through layers of self-importance, a lifetime of bourgeois privilege, and scraped the hard bone of pride: "Vanity of vanities; all is vanity." With those three words, so quietly and politely spoken, she had indirectly told me what the Catholic Worker Movement is all about and what she herself was like.[2]

Maybe truly ordinary individuals can be like this because they don't base their self-esteem on a distorted, narcissistic belief in their own accomplishments or image. They're not busy worrying about losing what they don't need. Consequently, they can be less defensive and more welcoming.

Another example of this type of attitude is contained in a story related by Norman Vincent Peale about Billy Graham.

During one of [Graham's] crusades in London, the British newspapers quoted some cutting remarks about him by a well-known clergyman of that country. It was reported that when someone began telling Billy about this, he said: "God bless that man. If I were in his place, I'd probably feel the same way about me."[3]

Peale notes how "such an attitude ensures personal peace of mind as well as the love and respect of other people. If only we could be that way more of the time."

Due to our lack of complete trust in God's revelation that we are made in the divine image and likeness, most of us get caught up in trying to be extraordinary. We become insecure and are tempted to rest our sense of self on something less than God's love for us. As a result, we waste our energy worrying about whether we are liked, respected, effective, or as good as other people.

We certainly can learn from Jesus' example in this regard. In contrast to our concern with what other people think of us, Jesus did not compare himself to others. We cannot find a single instance in the New Testament where he clung to his divinity. He wasn't obsessed with his image as we so often are with ours. Instead, he was only concerned with: 1) trying to be who he was called to be (obedience); 2) being in solidarity with others (community); 3) doing everything in the right Spirit (love). This is only possible for us when we, like Jesus, 1) feel deeply loved by God; 2) see the essential value and challenge of "simply" being ourselves (ordinary); 3) resist the temptation to create a false image of ourselves. Both our anxieties and the values of our society can seduce us into trying to develop, or hold onto, another image of self—even if it be a seemingly desirable or good one.

The Spirit of ordinariness invites each of us to follow the will of God by trying to find out what our inner motivations and talents are and then to express them without reserve or self-consciousness. This is true ordinariness. Although the call to be ordinary may be simple, it is not easy! And, because very few of us appreciate this subtle, yet profound, distinction, "being ordinary" is an extraordinary event in our times.

> A man traversed land and sea to check for himself the Master's extraordinary fame. "What miracles has your Master worked?" he said to a disciple. "Well there are miracles and miracles. In your land it is regarded as a miracle if God does someone's will. In our country it is regarded as a miracle if someone does the will of God."[4]

Another reason for the difficulty in trying to embrace our ordinariness is that each personal journey is uncharted. Another dialogue between a master and his disciple shows us how taking the time to reflect on our gifts and the sources of life for us can give us a sense of direction.

> [The disciple asked:] "What good work shall I do to be acceptable to God?" . . .

[The master answered:] "The Bible says that Abraham practiced hospitality and God was with him. Elias loved to pray and God was with him. David ruled a kingdom and God was with him too."

"Is there some way I can find my own allotted work?"

"Yes. Search the deepest inclination of your heart and follow it."[5]

As is the case with the call to simply be ourselves, listening to God through our own deep experiences of self is a basic lesson of spiritual discernment. Yet most of us don't do this. Instead, we often answer the secular calls to be successful, unique, secure, perfect, or right. We try to accomplish another goal which we believe will protect us from facing our dependence on God or keep us from experiencing life as a mystery we can't fathom or control. Maybe that is why one of the most essential challenges we face is to truly accept our limits. When we do this, the opportunity for personal growth and development is almost limitless. And, as we might expect, accepting our limits is not very popular. In fact, it is countercultural.

ORDINARINESS IS COUNTERCULTURAL

There is little call in the world today to "just be yourself." Only a few persons are graced with the freedom to recognize the waste and illusion of trying to be someone other than who they are called to be. As the poet e.e. cummings said: "to be nobody but yourself in a world which is doing its best, night and day, to make you everybody else means to fight the hardest battle which any human being can fight, and never stop fighting."

The attractiveness that modern society attributes to "success" and "importance" is very alluring. But ancient and contemporary philosophers and spiritual guides have not always viewed these goals positively. For instance, in 424 BC, Aristophanes, an Athenian poet, listed three essentials for climbing the ladder of success: "to plunder, to lie . . . (and) to show your arse!" Nine hundred years later, Abba Silvanus, an early desert father, warned: "Woe to you whose reputation is greater than your talents." This is quite different from the contemporary public relations philosophy which seeks to magnify people and products one-hundred fold to attract others to them, regardless of the reality. Exaggeration is the name of the game today. It has gotten so bad that in many situations we don't even know how to interpret the usual cues we get in today's hyperbolic society.

Recently, I heard a love song playing in the next room and went in to see if there was an old romantic movie being shown on TV which I might want to watch. It turned out to be an advertisement for hand soap!

Probably one of the most direct statements on the danger of pandering to the world in order to be noticed, appreciated, or admired was made by Thomas Merton. He said: "Be anything you like, be a madman, drunk, and bastard of every shape and form, but at all costs avoid one thing—success."[6] In this statement, he echoes Paul's famous line from Romans: "Do not conform yourself to this age but be transformed by the renewal of your mind, so that you may judge what is God's will, what is good, pleasing and perfect" (12:2). But, once again, it is easier said than done. Even when we think we are practicing ordinariness and humility, we often miss the mark. At least, I know that is often the case with me.

Several years ago I was trying to reach a colleague of mine who was a seminary dean. I wanted to ask him to review a manuscript I was preparing for publication. But when I called his office, the young person who answered told me that he was on sabbatical. Since I was constrained by time, I tried to find out if there were some way I could contact him. The longer I was on the phone with this individual, the more curt he seemed to get. Finally, in frustration I blurted out: "To whom am I speaking anyway?" The person replied in a very officious sounding voice: "This is *the* Reverend. . . ."

After the conversation was over, I related the story to a friend. I told her how furious and upset I was with the individual, what a poor representation of ministry he offered, how I was tempted to end the conversation with: "Well, when you're in touch with the dean will you please tell him *the* Doctor Wicks called!"

After my friend listened to my story, she smiled and said: "I wonder why you got so upset? I think I would probably have burst out laughing." Then the light dawned for me! I was complaining about him being pompous and not having humility, and was totally missing the fact that I was upset because my own very inflated ego was being attacked. I might have been frustrated in speaking with him, but if I were secure in myself, I would not have given the power away and taken his comment to heart. What lengths we go to in protecting our own brittle self-image!

Henri Nouwen relates an experience that has been helpful to me as I reflect on this incident. During his stay in a Trappist monastery in Genesee, New York, he would meet with the abbot John Eudes. In one session Nouwen discussed how the experience of rejection caused him not just a sense of irritation, but of deep hurt. As a result he was often plagued by ruminations of anger and revenge.

> The problem, [Eudes] said, is not that your feel-ings are totally illegitimate. In fact, you might have a good reason to feel rejected. But the problem is

that your response has no proportion to the nature of the event. In fact, the people you felt rejected by really don't mean that much to you. But little rejections like these open up a huge chasm, and you plunge right into it all the way to the bottom.

We tried to explore the reason for this fact. Somewhere there must be a need for total affection. . . . I keep hoping for a moment of full acceptance, a hope I attach to very little events. Even something rather insignificant becomes an occasion for this . . . and a small rejection then easily leads to a devastating despair and a feeling of total failure. John Eudes made it very clear how vulnerable I am with such a need because practically nobody can offer me what I am looking for (and) even if someone did offer me this . . . I would not be able to accept it since it would force me into an infantile dependency which I, as an adult, cannot tolerate.[7]

Our inordinate need to be loved can often make the image we have of ourselves quite brittle, leading us to overreact.

However, ordinariness, "just being yourself," should not be confused with passivity. It does not mean that when people present themselves to us in a negative way that we should not be assertive and say something. Passivity is no more of a virtue than aggressiveness. Like an inflated ego, it is also a sign of poor self-esteem; in theological terms, it is a failure to truly believe we are made in God's image and likeness. Too often we swallow pain and mistakenly call it virtue instead of recognizing it for what it is: unconscious and unnecessary fear of confrontation.

An incident that occurred a number of years ago taught me this lesson quite clearly. I remember walking down the hallway of the college where I was teaching and seeing a colleague standing just inside an office doorway. I stopped to pass the time of day and share some of the good things that were happening in my department. Everything I said seemed to elicit a sarcastic remark. Thinking I was being compassionate, I absorbed each negative response and tried to lighten the interaction with a humorous comment. Finally I thought: "Good grief. She certainly is in a terrible mood today. I'd better leave. I'm only making things worse!"

Several days later I related the incident to my best friend. "Well, what did you say to her about her behavior?" he asked. "I didn't say anything," I responded. Then I added (proudly . . . and yet humbly!), "I was not going to let her behavior affect my behavior."

Much to my surprise, my friend did not show great admiration for my wonderful "Christian" behavior. Instead, he said: "Well, you didn't really help her very much did you."

"I wasn't going to be sarcastic like she was," I responded defensively.

Undaunted, he then said: "I didn't say you had to be nasty in return, but you could have said: 'Gee, you seem to be coming across in a very strong and negative way. Did something I say key off your anger, or are you angry at someone or something else?' In this way you might have been able to help her with what she was troubled with at the time and surfaced any problems between the two of you."

He was right of course. Too often we miss opportunities to deal with conflict by opening up a subject for examination. Frequently, because of a lack of self-esteem, we fear other's anger and the possibility of a disagreement. We commit the sin of "chronic niceness" and then feel we have been virtuous. If my self-esteem at the time were more deeply rooted in trust in my covenant with God rather than dependent on my own image, I might have risked a confrontation. It certainly would have been more helpful than my (supposedly virtuous) silence. My friend's willingness to be honest helped me recognize even more how a lack of self-esteem prevents me from being ordinary and free in how I interact with others. It also made me see more clearly the connection between ordinariness and the positive feelings I have about myself.

ORDINARINESS AND SELF-ESTEEM

The beauty of the human being as part of creation has long been celebrated in sacred scripture:

> And God saw every thing that he had made, and, behold, it was very good (Gn 1:31, KJV).

> The earth is full of the goodness of the Lord (Ps 33:5, KJV).

> I am fearfully and wonderfully made (Ps 139:14, KJV).

What was written in the Hebrew scriptures is beautifully brought to completion in Jesus' statement: "You are my friends" (Jn 15:14).

Yet, there is much in us that seems to lack trust in this love. As the historian Neil Richardson once noted: "Jesus taught that God was not only more demanding than people cared to think, but also more generous than they dared to hope."[8] We must face this reality directly if we are to embrace ordinariness rather than exist in fear whether it be fear of falling from favor in the eyes of others or in our own estimation of self. Vincent Van Gogh once said: "The best way to know God is to love many things." *Especially* ourselves.

But love makes us vulnerable and we must be prepared for this. As C. S. Lewis understood:

> Love anything, and your heart will certainly be wrung and possibly broken. If you want to make sure of keeping it intact, you must give your heart

to no one, not even to an animal. Wrap it carefully round with hobbies and little luxuries; avoid all entanglements; lock it up safe in the casket or coffin of your selfishness. But in that casket—safe, dark, motionless, airless—it will change. It will not be broken; it will become unbreakable, impenetrable, irredeemable.

If we are to love—and this is our real *raison d'etre*—we must simultaneously love ourselves and allow ourselves to be deeply loved by God. Otherwise we will lead a see-saw existence, burdened by the weight of selfishness on the one hand and guilt over our failures on the other.

People say dreams sometimes contain opportunities to meet God; maybe the same can be said of daydreams. Given this, the following reverie might provide some insight into the delicate relationship between self-esteem and ordinariness, and between God's love and healthy love of self.

I was at home in my office, sitting on a small sofa, looking out the window. "I wonder what it would be like if I died right now?" I thought.

First I pictured myself in heaven, reporting my sins, and—being the type of person I am—making excuses for them. "If you would have been there Lord, I would *never* have done such terrible things!

Then, much to my surprise, God asked me to sit down. After listening to my confession of sins for a while longer, the Lord held up a hand for me to stop and looked at me in a quizzical but somewhat sad way. "You misunderstand. There's no need for all of your excuses. I am not angry with you."

I answered with a note of curiosity in my voice: "You're not?"

"No. But I am a little surprised and puzzled." Then God went on to say: "You see, I remember the exact moment when you were born. It was exciting! In the heavens, we got a thrill out of your creation. We were pleased. And so, the question I have for you now is: Why haven't *you* taken more time during your life to stand in wonder, awe, and gratitude for my presence within you?"

Even in my daydreams I am very defensive, so I responded: "Lord, I guess, I did not want to be guilty of the sin of narcissism."

To this comment, God responded: "When you are out on a hot sunny day and you feel a wonderfully cool breeze, do you enjoy it?"

"Why, yes."

"Can you control it?"

"No."

"Are you the source of it?"

"No."
"Is it your breeze?"
"No."
"Now, do you see what I mean?"

It was at that point that the daydream was over. As I sat there, I knew that I may have had the whole or most of the responsibility for the reverie. Consequently, I was concerned about deluding myself as I have so often done in the past. Yet, even with this proviso, I felt there was something to be learned from reflecting on it.

Somehow a message that I might have appreciated earlier in my life had once again returned to a conscious level of personal awareness and was reinforced for me. Although aware that I was not physically dead, I certainly felt both psychologically and spiritually lifeless. I knew I had forgotten Jesus' important message: "The kingdom of God is within you" (Lk 17:21). As a result, I frequently failed to appreciate my gifts in life. Thus I tried to run from my ordinariness and dependence on God with the thought: If I am to make it in this world I have to be successful *on my own*. How I had lacked trust in the Lord. How ungrateful to God I was . . . and still am!

What this reverie and subsequent reflection point out to me is the sad truth that I, and many others, are often "asleep (in life) with compasses in our hands."[9] We don't seem to realize that a full appreciation of our beautiful ordinariness can help wake us up to the gifts we have already been given by God. If only we would properly attend to God's gifts to us and in us! Then self-awareness and healthy self-love could form a positive circle of spiritual self-esteem and ultimately be a source of strength for others as well as ourselves. Will we have the trust to do this? Will we take the time?

Personal awareness of self before a loving God is also important because it helps self-confidence to grow and be more resistant to the assaults of failure or rebuff. Thus, it allows our character to develop and enables the presence of God within us to be felt in a good way by others. It is not that we forget or deny our faults; rather, we are better able to put them into perspective instead of being crushed by them.

As Rabbi Abraham Heschel observed: "Man sees the things that surround him long before he becomes aware of his own self. Many of us are conscious of the hiddenness of things, but few of us sense the mystery of our own presence."[10] Teresa of Avila, Francis of Assisi, and other spiritual figures were an exception to this. They had a real sense of self and manifested "pure presence." Due to their honesty, self-confidence, and lack of defensiveness, they let their personalities be felt to the fullest. Thus their sense of self had a wonderful impact on others, and many who encountered them directly were changed in the process.

But often our insecurities prevent us from being simply ourselves for others. A blind man once gave a eulogy for a famous Zen master named Bankei:

> Since I cannot see a person's face, I must judge his sincerity by his voice. Usually when I hear someone congratulate a friend on some success, I also hear envy in his voice, and when I hear expressions of condolence, I hear a secret tone of pleasure. Not so with Bankei; when he expressed happiness, his voice was completely happy, and when he expressed sadness, sadness was all I heard.[11]

This is what it really means to be oneself, to be ordinary: not to waste energy on subterfuge, defensiveness, envy, or competitiveness, but instead to be at ease with oneself and who one is. What a gift it is to be able to accept oneself and recognize the nobility of one's birth as a special creation! But do we really feel this way about ourselves?

To quote Heschel again:

> Verbally, we seem to be committed to the idea that man is created in the likeness of God. But are we committed to it intellectually? If the divine likeness is our premise, then the question arises: How should a being created in the likeness of God act, think, feel? How should we live in a way which is compatible with our being a likeness of God?[12]

These are the very questions we must face when we look at the connection between appreciation of our own ordinariness and the style we have of interacting with God, and nurturing God's presence in others.

ORDINARINESS AND COMPASSION

When ordinariness becomes the spiritual foundation of self-esteem, one of the fruits is the freedom to be in relationship with others in a healthy, loving, and helpful way. As St. Seraphim notes: "Acquire inward peace, and a multitude around you will find their salvation." Yet, until we reach this point, we may tend to be primarily concerned about our own image and thus be insecure, defensive, and judgmental. Consequently, even our love of other people will be limited and tied to our expectations of them.

As Henri Nouwen recognizes:

> It is important for me to realize how limited, imperfect, and weak my understanding of love has been. . . . My idea of love proves to be *exclusive*. "You only love me truly if you love others less;" *possessive*: "If you really love me, I want you to pay special attention to me;" and *manipulative*: "When you love me, you will do extra things for me." Well, this idea of love easily leads to *vanity*: "You must see something very special in me;" to *jealousy*: "Why are you now suddenly so interested in someone else and not in me?" and to *anger*: "I

am going to let you know that you have let me
down and rejected me."[13]

My point then is: To have healthy relationships
with others we must be clear about our relationship
with ourselves. Our relationship with self determines
how we will deal with the world. If we lack confidence, we may well interpret the actions and motivations of others inappropriately in a negative way and
react with unnecessary fear, anger, or distress. Rous-
seau once said: "The primary function of early education is to expand in children the faculty of wonder."
If we can appreciate the presence of God in ourselves
as we have been created, we will be more open to
finding God in others *as they are*. Consequently, we
will not have predetermined expectations of others'
behavior—even if they are very different, "alien," or
even "the enemy." Then we will love our neighbors
as ourselves; we will be in solidarity with others as a
unique people who are among the people of God.

As Merton correctly warned during the height of
the Vietnamese war:

Violence rests on the assumption that the
enemy and I are entirely different: the enemy is
evil and I am good. The enemy must be destroyed
and I must be saved. But love sees things differently. It sees that the enemy suffers from the same
sorrows and limitations that I do. That we both
have the same hopes, the same needs, the same

aspiration for a peaceful and harmless human life. And that death is the same for both of us. Then love may perhaps show me that my brother is not really my enemy and that war is both his enemy and mine. War is our enemy. Then peace becomes possible.[14]

If we are grateful and trusting enough to accept the God-given grace to see creation alive within us, we will then have the confidence, desire, and ability—even during the most difficult and conflictual of times—to see and embrace it in others as well. And, this can radically alter both our approach to life and the way we actually experience it.

The following story may clarify this point.

God decided to become visible to a king and a peasant and sent an angel to inform them of the blessed event. "O king," the angel announced. "God has deigned to be revealed to you in whatever manner you wish. In what form do you want God to appear?"

Seated pompously on his throne and surrounded by awestruck subjects, the king royally proclaimed: "How else would I wish to see God, save in majesty and power? Show God to us in the full glory of power."

God granted his wish and appeared as a bolt of lightning that instantly pulverized the king and his court. Nothing, not even a cinder, remained.

The angel then manifested herself to a peasant saying: "God deigns to be revealed to you in whatever manner you desire. How do you wish to see God?"

Scratching his head and puzzling a long while, the peasant finally said: "I am a poor man and not worthy to see God face to face. But if it is God's will to be revealed to me, let it be in those things with which I am familiar. Let me see God in the earth I plough, the water I drink, and the food I eat. Let me see the presence of God in the faces of my family, neighbors, and—if God deems it as good for myself and others—even in my own reflection as well."

God granted the peasant his wish, and he lived a long and happy life.[15]

May God grant all of us this same wish!

Two

LESSONS FROM THE DESERT

*P*robably no other group can teach us more about the spirit of ordinariness than the *abbas* and *ammas* (fathers and mothers) of the fourth and fifth century African and Persian deserts. After the conversion of the emperor Constantine and the proclamation of the Edict of Milan in 313 (which made Christianity legal), the church and the temporal order were reconciled. When this happened, the faith, rather than continuing to challenge the order of things, became domesticated. Moreover, its members no longer feared persecution and became more and more comfortable with the status quo.

As the church started to lose its prophetic character some people recognized that they too were in danger of becoming secularized and compromised in the process. These men and women took a very dramatic step: they went to the edge of civilization to sit with God in silence and solitude. In doing this, these "new pilgrims" set a dramatic example for both their own contemporaries and for later Christians who followed them into the "wilderness," either in fact or in spirit. What they all shared was a desire to find God by finding themselves. To do this, they asked for the grace to let go of the illusions and delusions upon which their identity had previously been based. They wished only to be themselves—to be ordinary.

Yet, this was no easy task. As these bearers of the spirit would come to recognize: "The longest journey is the journey inward." In addition, they also came to appreciate a parallel that would later be taught explicitly by Teresa of Avila: we find God by uncovering our own true selves; and it is in the search for God that we can better discover who we are. Through their appreciation of ordinariness, these spiritual guides realized intuitively what theologians call "the divinization of the human person." Psychologists now describe this as having a "solid self-esteem" that isn't swayed dramatically by the opinions or reactions of others.

These early spiritual guides sought to follow Jesus' example of going out to the desert to hear the word of God, to encounter temptations (Mt 4:1, Mk 1:12, Lk 4:1), and to "Come away to some lonely place all by yourselves and rest for a while" (Mk 6:31). As Thomas Merton recognized, the flight of these early pilgrims to the desert was "a refusal to be content with arguments, concepts, and technical verbiage. They sought a way to God that was uncharted and freely chosen, not inherited from others who had mapped it out beforehand. They sought a God whom they alone could find, not one who was given in a set, stereotyped form by somebody else."[16]

While their actions may seem extraordinary, as indeed they were, they still have a lot to teach us about being ordinary. The desert provided a place where it was difficult to hide from the most basic realities of ordinary Christian life. Thus they provide us with a model of fashioning our own ordinary way, a way that is for us "uncharted and freely chosen." In seeking to discover God and their own true identity, an additional unexpected grace emerged. Uncovering and valuing their own ordinariness enabled them to be free and strong enough to help others experience the simple presence of God in themselves. In other words, they became gentle and strong enough to be truly compassionate. To quote Merton again:

> These monks insisted on remaining human and "ordinary." This may seem to be a paradox, but it is very important. If we reflect a moment,

we will see that to fly into the desert in order to be extraordinary is only to carry the world with you as an implicit standard of comparison. The result would be nothing but self-contemplation, and self-comparison with the negative standard of the world one had abandoned. Some of the monks of the desert did this, as a matter of fact: and the only fruit of their trouble was that they went out of their heads. The simple men who lived their lives out to a good old age among the rocks and sands only did so because they had come into the desert to be themselves, their ordinary selves, and to forget a world that divided them from themselves. There can be no other valid reason for seeking solitude or for leaving the world.[17]

The threats to the spirit of ordinariness of the desert fathers and mothers of the fourth and fifth centuries are worth discussing here because they are in many ways similar to the ones we still face today.

Among these we must certainly include:

- the *projection* of blame onto others;

- a human tendency toward *callousness or deafness to the word of God*;

- duplicity: the temptation to unconsciously compromise with secular values.

These three are especially relevant because when they are present they distract us from embracing our ordinariness and drain off (or redirect) the energy necessary to uncover, develop or enhance our own true sense of self. Given this, they may seriously stunt both spiritual and personal maturity and undermine the self-esteem necessary to appreciate God's image reflected in ourselves. This may then prevent us from being in a good position to help foster strong Christian community among those with whom we live and work.

PROJECTION

Contemporary psychology points out how the primitive defense of "projection" operates beyond our level of awareness. Without knowing it, something we find emotionally unacceptable in us is rejected and attributed to or projected onto others. The "advantage" (secondary gain) of doing this is that we are able to give away the blame so we don't have to look at such difficulties or deficits within ourselves. The problem is, in giving away the blame, we also give away the power.

After all, if most things were more or less other people's fault, we would have little opportunity to improve, grow, and change. But by facing our projections, the energy we are wasting on defense can be reclaimed and made available for self-understanding and insight. Until we do this, our personalities are like well-fortified cities in which most of the resources are expended on exterior fortifications with little left to feed life within. Furthermore, where there is little energy or desire for self-understanding and appreciation of self, there is scant self-respect or self-esteem. As a result, this leaves the "psychological and spiritual doors" open to the dangers of manipulation by others. To enjoy being liked or appreciated by others is natural; there is nothing wrong with this. However, to need approval to feel complete as a person is to be in an overly dependent situation and this understandably may be quite dangerous.

The spiritual figures of the desert had an awareness of the special value of self-understanding and the importance of taking responsibility for one's own actions and mistakes, thirteen hundred years before psychology did. For them: "The demonic stood not merely for all that was hostile to [the human person]; the demons summed up all that was anomalous and incomplete in [people]."[18]

That such a view was central to the spirituality of this period in Christianity is quite understandable because the "father of the desert," Abba Anthony, held this belief close to his heart and modeled it for all who sought him out and tried to emulate his teachings and example. Accordingly:

It may come as a surprise to learn that St. Anthony of all people, thought the devil had some good in him. This was not mere sentimentalism. It showed that in Anthony there was not much room left for paranoia. We can profitably reflect that modern mass-man is the one who has returned so whole heartedly to fanatical projections of all one's own evil upon "the enemy" (whoever that may be). The solitaries of the desert were much wiser.[19]

Gale Marie Priestly helps us further understand this essential theme of Abba Anthony. She does this by offering a parallel between the sayings of the desert fathers and the psychology of the well-known Swiss psychiatrist Carl Jung:

Jung also recognized the inevitability of projections: "Projections change the world into a replica of one's own unknown face." Once a man has slowly developed this more complete vision of his true nature, a vision uncontaminated by dark projections, he "knows that whatever is wrong in the world is in himself." The desert fathers and Jung stand in close agreement in their recognition of the problem of projecting one's shadow and the necessity of withdrawing such projections as part of the spiritual way.[20]

An important distinction is necessary at this point: the desert fathers and mothers and Carl Jung are not commending a process of self-condemnation.

Such emotional self-flagellation is both unnecessary and self-destructive. They are saying that steps—and strong steps at times!—must be taken to withdraw our projections. Otherwise, as the following interaction implies, our desire for enlightenment will be stymied:

"What is the greatest enemy of Enlightenment?"
"Fear."
"And where does fear come from?"
"Delusion."
"And what is delusion?"
"To think that the flowers around you are poisonous snakes."
"How shall I attain Enlightenment?"
"Open your eyes and see."
"What?"
"That there isn't a single snake around."[21]

We must be willing to accept responsibility for our lives if we are to increase our own self-understanding and be open to a life that is honest and holy. Otherwise, if this doesn't occur, crucial opportunities for personal development may be delayed or lost. Consider the following vignette as an illustration of this point.

About six months after being fired from a position in ministry, a friend of mine was speaking with me about her feelings once again. (She had already previously discussed this situation with me three or four times since her employment had been terminated.) I was very much aware of what she was going through and was more sympathetic than I might normally have been because I too had experienced not having my contract renewed at an early point in my career.

I still remember my own response: I was full of anger and self-blame; I vacillated between unexpressed feelings of shame and loudly expressed notions of indignation and blame of others. Thankfully, I was eventually nudged by others to see as realistically as possible not only the shortcomings of others and the political situation I was up against, but also my own role in it.

So, when I thought the timing was right, after listening to her story once again, I responded. I tried to sum up all of the negative assessments she had made of others involved in her being let go. Then, I added: "You are at a point now at which you can see quite clearly the faults of those who were involved in terminating your position. You also have really begun to appreciate that despite your hurt, your anger, and your disappointment, your self-worth is certainly not measured by the evaluation of your performance by others. However, if you are to learn from this terrible situation, you must be open as well to see what role you played in making the situation better or worse. Do you think you are ready to think and speak about this?"

Psychologists are often called upon to tell people things they don't necessarily want to hear. Sensitive phrasing and good timing are essential. Otherwise the person may experience what is called a "narcissistic injury." This occurs when one feels deeply and personally hurt by the remark in a way that undermines self-esteem and/or causes one to erect a defensive wall to block self-examination. Such therapeutic interventions are designed to help make the "pre-conscious" (what is just beyond our level of awareness) more conscious and thus more available to people. This makes a fuller self-understanding more possible.

In this case, I thought the timing was right for the step I took. However, as it turned out, I was wrong. Instead of accepting the possibility of her own complicity in the problem, she maintained she had no role whatsoever in her being fired and that it was totally their fault.

Since then, months have passed and she has begun seeing a bit more of her role in the overall interpersonal dynamic of what occurred. But she still remains mostly in the dark. Hopefully this will change as her self-confidence grows, as she becomes more open, and when someone like me intervenes again—maybe this time when the timing is better and she is stronger and more able to deal with the pain that often accompanies such efforts at self-discovery.

None of us likes to look at our role in the problems we encounter. As my daughter reminds me when she hears me complaining about how difficult it is for me to hear the things necessary for my own personal growth: "Dad. No pain, no gain!" (Imagine having to sit and listen to such truths from your own daughter!) Or, as a friend of mine says: "I've never met a projection I didn't like."

It is obvious that the desert fathers and mothers knew this and that one of their main goals and methods was to deal with the natural tendency to project one's own sins onto others. They felt that in silence and solitude, in listening to God when one is alone, there must be a willingness to do everything possible to face oneself honestly and directly. They recognized that not to do so would be tragic not only for them, but also for anyone who might be in need of their compassionate help. Such self-examination and self-awareness is an integral part of the ordinariness that is the foundation of self-esteem.

Knowing this helps us to better understand their motives for going apart and we see more clearly the relevancy of their messages for us today. As Kenneth Leech notes: "The protest of the solitary is not against human companionship as such, but against the evasion of self which can easily occur when involvement with people obscures and prevents any real encounter with one's own identity. Only in *stillness* can the truth be seen."[22]

CALLOUSNESS

When we sit prayerfully in silence and solitude we are entering the desert, our desert. In this sacred space, the goal is not to hide from others, devoid of pain, or to hold ourselves apart from and above the community in which we live. It is to receive the grace to learn to face ourselves directly so we can learn to live ordinariness, to live ethically and generously with others.

The following little story illustrates how well the desert fathers and mothers knew about the value of silence and solitude:

> In Scetis, a brother went to see Abba Moses and begged him for a word. And the old man said: "Go and sit in your cell, and your cell will teach you everything."[23]

The existentialist Albert Camus also recognized this:

> When a man has learned—and not on paper—how to remain alone with his sufferings, how to overcome his longing to flee, then he has little left to learn.

Henri Nouwen saw this as well:

> We have, indeed, to fashion our own desert where we can dwell in the gentle healing presence of our Lord. [Prayer] challenges us to hide

absolutely nothing from God and to surrender ourselves unconditionally to his mercy.[24]

Yet, rarely do we pray faithfully this way. Indeed, many of us would prefer to read about the spiritual life rather than live it. We prefer to hear and repeat others' prayers than to utter our own deeply felt urgings when sitting in silence and spending time alone with God.

On first blush, this seems puzzling. After all why do we create so many reasons not to pray if a relationship with God can free us to relate more openly with ourselves and others? It doesn't seem reasonable. On the other hand, when we take the time to examine the resistances to prayer more closely, we can see that such hesitancies to meet God in honesty, silence, and solitude are related to numerous factors. Among them are not wanting to let go in order to see ourselves and our behavior in an unvarnished way; and not having enough courage and trust in God to drop our defenses so we can be nothing more or less than who we were created to be—our ordinary selves.

Therefore, although taking fifteen or twenty minutes to be with God each day in silence and solitude sounds good (and easy in theory), the reality is obviously very different. When you ask most people (even those who would readily admit that such an activity is important) whether they actually take time with God in stillness each day, they, like most of us, would probably admit they hold prayer in high esteem but are not faithful to it.

One of the reasons for this is that quiet, honest prayer is often unnerving. So, unconsciously knowing this leads many of us to develop a schedule in which we become too active to slow down and too full to make room for God. In an effort to run from our sense of emptiness and utter dependence on God, our minds become filled with anxieties and worries, our hearts heavy with actual or imagined losses in our lives, and our spirits weighed down with angers, hurts, and a sense that no one really understands.

To make matters worse, these are the idols we must then bring into our quiet time if and when we do allot such time to be with God alone. And so, when we stop to pray, instead of our hearts opening up to the Lord, our minds open up to our own fragmented world within. When we close our eyes, what happens? Is it an opportunity to hear the hopeful message of God, or a time to be bombarded by preoccupations and worries? Is it not true that these preoccupations arise out of our desire to control a world of our own making—a comfortable one that is really artificial, dead, and full of denial? It is a world that keeps us enveloped in security until the threat of our own actual physical death awakens us to the sad recognition of our long years of spiritual rigor mortis. We feel that in trying to master our own fate, we are prepared for neither life nor death.

We seem to know that to be centered in life is to have everything we think, say, and do be an outgrowth of an attitude connected with our deepest creative urgings. But most of us still live out the precious moments of our lives in reaction to our secret fears and shames. What a pity it is to be puppets and run each day toward our eventual death addicted, bored, anxious, angry, frustrated, resentful, and under the stress of our self-centered and reinforced negativity. How much sadder it is to do this while all the time believing we are just "being sensible" and "acting responsibly." We are called instead by Christ to be spontaneously alive in the Spirit.

To deal with such resistances, when we enter prayer the first commitment must be to "just" stay put, not run away, and be disciplined and regular in our attention to our time with God. When we are faithful we may initially feel somewhat lost and "between things." This is good in a way. It is like stretching to wake up—wake up in this case to the fact that we don't feel like we have God in our lives. The alternative to accepting the fact that we are all beginners at prayer and need to continually live with the awkwardness that comes with being dependent upon God is worse. For without quiet time in the morning or evening to slowly make our trust in God more visible, we tend to drift between guilt and impulse. And "drifting" is far different from "flowing." Drifting has no purpose, no divine theme; flowing with life is prayerfully being free and at home in the present, no matter what happens. Even when spiritual darkness and boredom occur during these periods, with prayer they lose their threat, become somewhat irrelevant, and (more importantly) are eventually passing experiences if only, as Abbot John Eudes suggests, we stay with our prayer:

> In the beginning, your thoughts will wander, but after a while you will discover that it becomes easier to stay quietly in the presence of the Lord. If your head seems filled with worries or concerns, you might like to start with some psalms or a scripture reading that can help you to concentrate and then you will be better prepared for silent meditation. When you are faithful in this, you will slowly experience yourself in a deeper way. Because in this useless (time) in which you do nothing "important" or "urgent," you have to come to terms with your basic powerlessness, and have to feel your fundamental inability to solve your or other people's problems or to change the world. When you do not avoid that experience but live through it, you will find out that your many projects, plans, and obligations become less urgent, crucial, and important and lose their power over you. They will leave you free during

> your time with God and take their appropriate
> place in your life.[25]

When Henri Nouwen received this very advice from the abbot during his stay at Genesee, his honest response was: "It seems very convincing to me, even obvious. The only task left is this: simply doing it in obedience." I would add—knowing my own sinfulness—doing it with tenancy!

As the author of *Theologia Germanica* says, "Nothing burns in hell but the self." The same can be said of the delusions and illusions we have about ourselves during our quiet times alone with God. In this empty period, the distractions are unveiled for what they are; the negative feelings and doubts we have suppressed start to rise to the surface, and we feel lost and unprepared to meet God. In these prayerful moments we see the charlatanism in our lives and recognize that our efforts to reach out to family, friends, and those in need have often been based more on comparison than compassion; we have forsaken our ordinariness for some other apparently attractive image which we then want others to appreciate.

During prayer we also face the judgmental attitudes we often keep carefully hidden under a veneer of "chronic niceness" when interacting with those we meet. In such instances, although our voice may be muted and we think we are being virtuous, our hearts are far from silent and accepting of others. Abba Poemen, a wise desert father, saw this and said: "There is one sort of person who seems to be silent, but inwardly criticizes other people. Such a person is really talking all the time. Another may talk from morning 'til night, but says only what is meaningful."[26] True prayer exposes this unpleasant reality to us.

Likewise, the attachments we have also unconsciously hidden may begin to surface when we encounter God during periods of silence and solitude (as well as when we share the fruits of these prayerful times with spiritual friends in our lives). However, the effort to meet God is worth the discomfort, pain, and tears, for without such honest prayer we may well miss important sources of knowledge about what blocks us from experiencing the fullness of the Lord (Jn 10:10) or stops us from being formed by God in an ongoing way in life (Rom 12:2). The following dialogue clearly stresses this point:

"Where can I find God?"
"He's right in front of you."
"Then why do I fail to see him?"
"Why does a drunkard fail to see his home?
Find out what it is that makes you drunk.
To see you must be sober."[27]

Knowing this, why do we still try to ignore the pristine loneliness of the moments of stillness we are being called to experience with God? Or, more pointedly, knowing true prayer is like planting a tree to help purify the stagnation of sin in our lives, why don't we spend more time in silence and solitude and give the loneliness we often experience a chance to blossom? In this way, the negative feelings and hidden denials deep within can rise and perch in front of us so we can address them with a God who loves us.

Why do we continually fail to see that the chance for real joy is wrapped in unexamined anger, apathy, and confusion? Why do we frequently miss the fact that our peace is shrouded in a fog of anxiety and preoccupation? When will we realize that if we stay with these feelings and worries, they will clear, and amidst the pain and joy of life we will find Truth, we will find God?

Maybe another partial answer to these questions lies in the fact that many of us fail to appreciate the dynamic interpersonal aspect of prayer. In silence and solitude we must do more than sit quietly and moodily waiting for God to perform for us in a way we would like. Prayer is a time of real relationship—a place where we can find that what may appear to be a foolish waste of time to persons involved in undisciplined activitism can actually be a journey into a deeper encounter with the living God.

As Metropolitan Anthony of Sourozh appreciates:

> First of all, it is very important to remember that prayer is an encounter and a relationship, a relationship which is deep, and this relationship

cannot be forced either on us or on God. If we
could mechanically draw him into an encounter,
force him to meet us, simply because we have
chosen this moment to meet him, there would be
no relationship and no encounter. We can do that
with an image, with the imagination, or with the
various idols we can put in front of us instead of
God; we can do nothing of that sort with the living God, any more than we can do it with a living
person.[28]

And so, it seems clear that too often what destroys
our relationship with God and makes us avoid disciplined, regular prayer are a lack of openness during
such periods and a predetermined idea of how God
should respond to us during our quiet time (which
only leads to discouragement when prayer doesn't
turn out as we would have it). The problem is we only
say that we want to be totally honest and naked before
God, that we want to be released from those troubles
or areas of ignorance that prevent us from being spiritually and psychologically healthy. In reality, we aren't
interested in listening to God, so our claims often lack
real substance. And the shallow content and lack of
intensity in our prayer reveal this fact.

After all, realistically, how often are we willing to
sit down, read a few lines of scripture or a good spiritual book, and wait in silence, letting the silence itself
speak to us rather than seeking the words we want
to hear? In truth, isn't the following prayer a better

reflection of what we are really saying to God in many instances?

Dear Lord, I am here to be with you as I truly am. I hold nothing back. I reveal all to you without reservation. Of course we won't speak about my problems with drinking. And there's no need for us to reflect on how vain and self-centered I am. Also, we don't need to go into the grudges I hold, the righteousness I feel toward some people, the embarrassment I experience when I think of some of the shameful things I've done or felt, or the times I have let down my friends, family, and those who count on me.

Now, of course, if you want to miraculously heal me so I can avoid the pain of self-confrontation, that's great! After all, you are God. But I don't want to talk about it myself or face anything really meaningful because I don't want to feel uncomfortable or dependent on you. I also don't want to come out of my secure little world onto the water to meet you as Peter did. Nor do I want to go into your dark night where I will feel so out of control and so dependent on your total love.

Let's face it, I even doubt your existence at times and don't really trust you; in my heart I feel that if anything good has happened to me it was primarily because I did it alone without any help from you. As a matter of fact, I'm only praying

> to you now because I've taken care of everything
> important today, because it's a habit, and to "cover
> my bets" in case you really do have the power. I
> guess down deep my lukewarm feeling is: "maybe
> prayer can't help, but it can't hurt." So I do it
> whenever there is nothing else to do or I feel I
> need a miracle to get what I want.

If this is our attitude, we must face a reality: if we want to have the passion and single-heartedness of the desert dwellers, God must become as real to us as the problems and joys we face each day. We must really want to pray, meet God, and uncover the strength of our ordinariness. We must be willing to let grace uncover, and help us face, our duplicity (Mt 6:24). Otherwise, God will remain on the outside and other values will be at the center ruling us in both obvious and unconscious ways.

DUPLICITY

Duplicity is the temptation to unconsciously compromise with secular values. As a threat to our true identity, it goes hand-in-hand with both "projection" and a failure to listen to God in stillness and solitude. The desert fathers and mothers knew this and struggled with lures to give up the purity of Christianity or to be someone other than the ordinary person God created them to be. They recognized how deeply what we would call secularism could infect their lives and values even if there was a feeling (and some public commitment) that God was the center of their lives.

Today secularism is particularly reflected in advertising which is so effective in appealing to our needs, even though what is offered can never fill the void left by the absence of God. To understand the severity of this problem is to appreciate how the psychology of advertising has often supplanted a theology of hope. We are more interested in possessing than in living in freedom. We believe that things, image, success, or being liked will make us secure, comfortable, and strong. We often confuse freedom with a so-called "freedom to choose." We let other people determine for us what our needs are rather than listening to our hearts' desire and allowing hope to grow. Consequently, we run through life trying to grasp what they tell us will fill us and make us whole.

> Publicity speaks in the future tense and yet the achievement of this future is endlessly deferred. How then does publicity remain credible—or credible enough to exert the influence it does? It remains credible because truthfulness of publicity is judged, not by the real fulfillment of its promises, but by the relevance of its fantasies to those of the spectatorbuyer. Its essential application is not to reality but to daydreams. No two dreams are the same. Some are instantaneous, others prolonged. The dream is always personal to the dreamer. Publicity does not manufacture the

> dream. All that it does is to propose to each one of
> us that we are not yet enviable—yet could be.[29]

Henri Nouwen, who is steeped in the wisdom of the desert, offers a parallel concern. In reflecting on secularism he carries the issue further when he addresses it to those in ministry who believe and claim they are living deeply committed Christian lives. He helps us see that no one is immune to the threat of secularism:

> I wonder if under the surface of our religios-
> ity we do not have great doubts about God's
> effectiveness in our world, about his interest in
> us—yes, even about his presence among us. I
> even wonder if there are many religious people
> for whom God is their only concern. When we
> speak of our age as a secular age, we must first of
> all be willing to become aware of how deeply this
> secularism has entered into our own hearts and
> how doubt, hesitation, suspicion, anger, and even
> hatred corrode our relationship with God.[30]

In periods of silence and solitude in our desert, in our effort to embrace ordinariness, Nouwen's questions and challenges must be faced.

AWARENESS OF GOD'S PRESENCE

So, where does knowing all of this leave us? What have we learned from the desert fathers and mothers (and the contemporary spiritual figures who have followed them into the "desert") about embracing ordinariness as the spiritual foundation of self-esteem and compassion? What can we do so our prayer doesn't turn out to be a mere fantasy in which we use up all of our energy on dreaming of holiness instead of living a life of true vision based on honest prayer and social action that lead to a real and strong relationship with God? Some final summary lessons from the fourth and fifth century desert fathers and mothers may help to answer these questions.

Prayer. The first lesson of ordinariness from the desert pilgrims is to actually take the time and energy to seek to experience the living God—not just to talk or think about prayer and call that the basis of a real relationship with the Lord. The following dialogue may help illustrate this point:

> A brother came to see Abba Theodore, and started to talk and inquire about things he himself had not tried yet. The old man said to him: You have not found a boat, or put your oars into it, and you haven't even sailed, but you seem to have arrived in the city already! Well do your work first; then you will come to the point you are thinking about now.[31]

Therefore, if we are to become prayerful people, our hearts and minds must come together each day in silence and solitude. Otherwise, we may come to discover nice things about God, but not really come to know the living God on a deep level.

An analogy may help to illustrate this point. If an alcoholic comes in to see me for psychological treatment and I only help him to intellectually understand why he became an alcoholic, what will this accomplish? If he doesn't come to a point in which his heart and head come together and lead to a commitment and subsequent action to stop drinking so he can open up his life to new freedom and self-respect, little will really change in his life. He will merely leave therapy as an "enlightened alcoholic" who will continue to drink.

And so, when people ask how they can begin a true prayer life once again, one suggestion can be safely offered: without fail begin every day by actually spending time quietly in silence, solitude, and meeting God in prayer. In this way, each day is centered on God and we become slowly more involved in the desire for a deep relationship with God.

When asked how long a period of time this should be, the answer I give (which usually causes some mild surprise) is: "Set a goal of ten to twenty minutes but always spend at least two minutes." This is often received with skepticism because people generally feel they owe much more time to God than that (which of course is true), and they often make such comments to me. My response is: "If you are anything like me, despite your good intentions, I don't trust that you will do it on a regular basis; yet, simple constant deeds are always more meaningful than rarely fulfilled great promises of fidelity. Besides, in time, a faithful schedule of a few moments of daily prayer will set the stage for a more mature relationship with God in which more time will be desired and spent in stillness with the Lord."

When we start each day by sitting down with our morning coffee or tea to spend some brief quiet time with the Lord, God's grace will lead us into greater divine union. Moreover, even on the busiest of days, this modest beginning is worthwhile because we cannot so easily shunt our time with God aside with the excuse: "Oh, I'm in too much of a rush; I'll pray later." After all, it is only two minutes and one of these days there simply will be no later!

So, when I am tempted to avoid even my two minutes with God, I think: "I can spend at least this little time with the Lord so the rest of my hectic schedule is driven by the right Spirit." And if I still resist it, I recall the way one of my elderly aunts responded to me anytime I would ask her about whether she was planning to attend a future event or not. If it were a long time off, she would say she didn't know if she would be alive to go to it. Whereas, if I asked her what she was going to do tomorrow, she never hesitated to tell me about her full schedule without a hint of a doubt that she would be able to be there for each and every event.

Just like her I deny my death by believing tomorrow will always come for me. And just like her some day I shall miss my next day's appointments. Is it any wonder then that the desert fathers carefully followed Christ's admonition to always keep death before your eyes?

Detachment. Another point from the desert that will help us to find and embrace our true, ordinary selves is detachment. Detachment is the need to uncover our compulsions and attachments in life so we can let go of our idols and risk meeting God anew each day. Once again, while this sounds great, it is not often practiced by us today. The paradox is: "We often complain the most about a lack of spiritual passion at the very time when we are willing to risk the least."[32]

Merton reflected on this very point in his study of the desert pilgrims. He writes:

> We cannot do exactly what they did. But we must be as thorough and as ruthless in our determination to break all spiritual chains, and cast off the domination of alien impulses, to find our true selves, to discover and develop our inalienable spiritual liberty and use it to build, on earth, the kingdom of God. This is not the place in which to speculate what our great and mysterious vocation might involve. That is still unknown. Let it suffice for me to say that we need to learn from these [people] of the fourth century how to ignore

> prejudice, defy compulsion, and strike out fear-
> lessly into the unknown.[33]

Truth. The theme of "truth" is at the heart of the spiritual life both in their time and ours. As Abraham Heschel, the great rabbi, would recognize many years after the treks of these men and women into the desert:

> Only one question is worthy of supreme anxi-
> ety: How to live in a world pestered with lies and
> remain unpolluted, how not to be stricken with
> despair, not to flee but to fight and succeed in
> keeping the soul unsoiled and even aid in purify-
> ing the world?[34]

Maybe that is why I think Sigmund Freud was more "spiritual" than Carl Jung. Jung may have been more "religious," but Freud was known for his relentless and fearless search for the truth. His conclusions have in many cases turned out to be wrong or unfounded but (as can be seen especially reflected in the novel on his life, *Passions of the Mind*) no one can fault him for cowardice in his search for what is true about the human person and his or her motivations in life.

Modeling ourselves after searchers for the truth, while good, is, once again, not easy. Too often I think we remain somewhat neurotic in life because of this. We would rather gather the crosses (that frequently come from an unnecessary preoccupation about the future of our life and the lives of others) which we feel we can carry (and control) rather than to remain hopeful and faithful with arms open to receive the crosses God may want to give us, whatever they may be. We are afraid to be free enough to see and live out the truths in life. Because our self-esteem is not based on ordinariness but on the image we and others have created, we are too sensitive to anything that might diminish it and make us face our frailty. But we must be strong.

Maybe this is what was in the mind of one of the abbas of the desert when he asked a disciple of his: "Tell me what you see in me and in turn I will tell you what I see in you." His disciple responded by saying: "You are good in soul, but a little harsh." To this, the old man responded: "And you are good, but your soul is not tough."[35] The message for us in the same. When facing fears, don't panic; when hearing negative feedback, don't lose a sense of God's love; when feeling a desire to pull back from God and avoid quiet prayer, be tough, stay with it in patience, perseverance, and with an open heart.

Scripture. The Jesuit philosopher Bernard Lonergan once noted: "Religious experience at its roots is an experience of an unconditional and unrestricted being in love. But what we are in love with remains something we have to find out." A fourth point from the desert which is in line with this statement is that in addition to quiet prayer, there must be a real commitment to undertaking a daily period of *lectio divina* with sacred scriptures. As Kenneth Leech notes:

> The Desert Fathers held, with Epiphanius
> of Cyprus, that "ignorance of the scriptures is a
> precipice and a deep abyss." They used the Psalms
> constantly. Their prayer was utterly and pro-
> foundly biblical. The contemplation of God was
> inseparable from the response to God's word in
> revelation, and the deep, inner struggle with the
> heart involved the interiorizing and digesting of
> the scriptures.[36]

Still, how many of us greet each day or relax for a few minutes in the evening with the scriptures? Yet, without meeting God each day in scripture our sense of God becomes too vague and open to our own musings or the tyranny and erratic impulses of our unconscious. Despite the value of frequent encounter with God in the scriptures, we might avoid reading them because we are only used to picking them up as part of a religious obligation (i.e., to write a homily, or as part of attending liturgy). In such times of formal attention to scriptures, it is easy to forget how wonderful it is to open a contemporary translation of the Bible (such as *The New Oxford Annotated Bible*, the *New Jerusalem Bible*, or the *New American Bible*), and to savor the words by reading a bit each day for nourishment and awakening. We have become bored by the scriptures.

We have forgotten that they can hold new inspiration for us if only we live with them each day and read the word with an attitude of freshness and quiet desire.

To demonstrate how serious a problem this has become, we need only reflect on our own lives or poll other Christians and ask: "Do you begin each day with a few minutes of quiet prayer and end your day with a reading of scriptures?" Few will answer in the affirmative. And, to see further how deep the resistance is to meeting God this way, set up a schedule of only seven minutes of prayer and scripture reading (two minutes of prayer in silence and solitude in the morning; five minutes of sitting and relaxing with scriptures in the evening) and see how hard it is to be faithful to it. (Talking about God is always easier than being with God in an intentional way.)

The depressing and yet hopeful part about this is something I see in my clinical practice with my patients, most of whom are in ministry. I have rarely seen a vowed religious, priest, or Protestant minister under psychological stress or experiencing burnout who had not also let his or her prayer disappear or be clouded over by a life of undisciplined activism. On the other hand, I have also witnessed the constant miracle of the seven minutes with God. The brief quiet time in the morning and short scripture reading in the evening have restored life to these people again and again. God's grace begins to help them see how they were not centered because they had put their "spiritual and psychological hands" around someone or something less than God's will. And, with prayer and reflection, their social action and religious leadership, as well as their times of leisure became richer because they now gave to others with a different motivation. They had a surfeit of peace even when they felt confused or in pain. Like Jesus, they gave "not to be loved, but because they were love." Only seven minutes; it's simple but, for many reasons, not easy and rarely practiced in a consistent way.

Wonder and Awe. We have seen how the desert fathers and mothers taught us to be truthful with ourselves so we know who we are in our ordinariness, to be prayerful each morning so we can take our relationship with God into each day, and to read and embrace the scriptures in the evening for a few minutes. To all of this we might add one more essential thing: Start each day anew with a deep sense of wonder and awe. In other words, meet life without preconceived notions or demands, with "low expectations and high hopes."

Without knowing it, Edmund Fuller in his book *Men in Modern Fiction* seemed to sum up this final theme from the desert (on the need for a sense of wonder and awe) when he wrote:

> The new gullibility of our particular time is not that of the man who believes too much, but that

of the man who believes too little—the man who has lost his sense of the miracle—the man capable of believing that creation is in some way an automatic or commonplace thing, or even that man himself, physically and psychically can be dissected into neat packages susceptible to complete explanation.

When awe and wonder depart from our awareness, depression sets in, and after its blanket has lain smotheringly upon us for a while, despair may ensue, or the quest for kicks begin. The loss of wonder, of awe, of the sense of the sublime, is a condition leading to the death of the soul. There is no more withering state than that which takes all for granted, whether with respect to human beings or the rest of the natural order. The blasé attitude means spiritual, emotional, intellectual, and creative death.[37]

Sensitivity to the presence of God in self and others and during those precious moments of prayerful stillness is not a nicety. It is:

- a responsibility of living,

- a graced appreciation of the fact that what is real and ordinary is a sanctuary for the sacred, a chance to meet God,

- a special chance to embrace the spiritual self-esteem that can only come from being gratefully aware of the unique divine presence in us,

- an invitation to go forward with others and compassionately build a world that is truly a gentle place for all of us to grow together before God.

And isn't this what ordinary life, the truly spiritual life, is supposed to be all about?

Part Two

SELF-ESTEEM

Three

WHAT IS MY TRUE FACE?

*I*n the last chapter we learned some lessons about ordinariness from the *abbas* and *ammas* of the early church who found God by finding themselves. We saw how projection, deafness to the word of God, and duplicity can keep us from embracing ordinariness. These failings can also be seen as symptoms of our need to strengthen our self-esteem. When we have a healthy sense of ourselves, we are willing to accept responsibility for our own actions, we are open to God's call to grow, and we are honest about our tendency to compromise.

A healthy self-esteem is essential for accepting our ordinariness. It is described by some as "the reputation you have with yourself."[38] And although this definition is helpful, it still leaves us with a number of important questions to face. Namely:

- How did I get this reputation?

- How accurate are my beliefs about myself?

- Is the reflection I see in "my mind's eye" really my "*true* face?"

Addressing these questions is crucial; our responses can determine how we will lead the rest of our lives. If these questions remain unaddressed or go unexamined, we may well end up traveling through life on psychological and spiritual "automatic pilot," guided by unarticulated beliefs or unconscious "voices" from our past which do not actually tell us the whole truth about ourselves.

The result will be a life where our basic intuition about ourselves and our whole way of living will lack the peace and strength that should be ours as friends of God (Jn 15:15). We actually keep ourselves from taking our necessary place at the table of life and therefore prevent ourselves from being fully alive in the Spirit. Moreover, such erroneous negative perceptions of self may interfere with our being full participants in fostering a just and loving world. Having a distorted self-image and resultant poor self-esteem is a serious problem; it can have detrimental consequences of a social and personal nature.

HOW DID I GET MY SELF-IMAGE?

When we were very young we looked into the faces of our parents, day care workers, older siblings, and friends to see our reflection. Ideally, their eyes reflected their unconditional love and acceptance of us. This should then have encouraged our enthusiasm for life and helped us to see the loving face of God in others. If so, then we did not make our self-worth contingent upon performance. Realistically though, our parents and significant others in our lives were "only human," and had needs of their own which were never completely met. They often came from situations that were far from perfect; the love and acceptance they received in their early years was not always unconditional. Without knowing it (or consciously trying to be malicious), our parents and the other significant people in our lives projected some of their own needs and demands onto us; because of this, their acceptance was conditional.

To make matters more complicated, we also introjected (took into ourselves unconsciously) some of the self-esteem deficits our significant others might have had at the time. Because they were our guides, we followed them in ways that were rarely spoken about—but which were subtly modeled by them and quickly learned by us! This mimicry was so imprinted then that we may still follow them to this day without knowing it! Here we find the truth of the saying "The apple doesn't fall far from the tree." (After all, how many times have we said to ourselves: "I can't believe I'm doing this! My parents used to say this when I was a child!")

The problem then is that we pick up styles of acting and negative messages about ourselves without even knowing it. These messages were frequently transmitted pre-verbally (before we had mastery of spoken language), nonverbally, and indirectly. Thus they are hard to uncover, evaluate, and correct, even if they are false. It is not unusual to hear people say: "I know I am a good person. I know I have many talents and people respect me. But when I do something wrong or someone says something negative about me, it seems to undo all of the positives. I believe the negative comment represents how people really feel about me and what I really believe to be true about myself." Such comments reveal a loyalty to some negative image of self, to a self-defeating role or way of thinking learned early in life.

In most cases, unless we see what is happening, this negative "music" will continue to play in our minds. We will react and submit to it all of our lives without even knowing it. For, as Virginia Woolf recognized: "It is far harder to kill a phantom than reality."[39]

In some cases the messages may be so distorted that a person needs therapy to rework the early relationships he or she has had:

> What becomes a person's self-esteem—his sense of cohesion and worthwhileness—is developed through empathic transactions with his parents. When parents' empathy for their child fails significantly, the result is defensive behavior with which the child seeks to protect himself from further frustration, hurt, disappointment, overstimulation, and so on. These defenses and their offshoots, if not satisfactorily resolved, later form the problematic aspects of an individual's character. If that person becomes a [therapy] patient he will sooner or later reenact in some fashion with the therapist the trauma of his earlier years, usually in response to a real or imagined failure in the therapist's empathy. If the patient's subsequent defensive behavior is . . . recognized for what it is, its examination can lead to an understanding of the earlier struggle that the patient is unsuccessfully trying to resolve in his present life.[40]

Informal forms of self-reflection, feedback from friends, family, and colleagues, and structured interactions with therapists, counselors, or spiritual guides are helpful ways of checking the accuracy of our view of ourselves. This is especially important with respect to the validity of any negative views we have of ourselves. Such interactions can be beneficial in supporting continued spiritual and psychological development. The psychiatrist Alfred Adler recognized many years ago that the private logic created in childhood may not be sufficient to carry us through adulthood with the vitality and peace we desire.

Women's self-esteem problems may also be "largely the result of female oppression in a male-dominated culture and society."[41] A similar statement could be made about "persons of color" in a primarily Caucasian society. So there are not only problems created by the understandable lacks within our family and inner circle of friends, there are also problems caused by prejudice and oppression within society which leads to diminishment of self-esteem. As the authors of *Beyond Sugar and Spice* point out:

> Certainly there are many women who have escaped the blight, who have lived full and happy lives, but when you leaf through the studies you can sense, floating in the air, ghosts of unborn dreams, unrealized hopes, undiscovered talents. The tragedies are the "might have beens," and they are the most poignant.[42]

In a comment made by the character Shirley Valentine (from the movie of the same name) we can see a similar theme poignantly made at one point as she is sitting by the seaside in Greece, reflecting on her own life and how "little" and "unused" it has been in many respects. She says:

I've allowed myself to lead a little life while inside me there was so much more . . . it's gone unused and now it never will be. Why do we get all this life if we never use it? Why do we get all these feelings and dreams and hopes if we don't ever use them. Dreams. They are never in the place you expect them to be.[43]

"Solidifying" one's self-esteem or finding one's true face is not something unhappy people with poor self-images can do by themselves. Nor is valuing ourselves deeply just a self-serving activity. To the contrary, correcting self-image and increasing self-esteem is something we must do for ourselves and for each other. Furthermore, we must do it *together*. If we really believe women, men, and people of all colors are the *imago Dei* (image of God), then the failure to seek the reflection of God in oneself or others' self-image is wrong, unjust . . . maybe even sinful.

WHAT IS MY TRUE FACE?

A philosopher of ancient times, Epictetus, once said: "You are a principal work, a fragment of God himself, you have in yourself a part of him. Why then are you ignorant of your high birth?"

In saying this, he is echoing a theme that we see in sacred scripture. In the Book of Genesis for instance it says: "God saw all he had made, and indeed it was very good" (1:31). Then, later in the New Testament we are told by Jesus in so many different ways that we are his "family" and his "friends" and are constantly reminded about his love for us. At one point, he even says the dramatic words: "The kingdom of God is within you" (Lk 17:21, KJV).

Yet, despite the Bible affirmation that we are created in the image and likeness of God, we don't seem to appreciate that God loves us for who we are as real people (our "ordinary" selves). Instead we seem to reject our birthright at times. We move through the world feeling bad about ourselves (because of our mistakes and sins), and we forget about God's deep love—a love that should be the solid basis of a self-esteem which would enable us to form sound relationships with others.

Maybe part of the reason for this is that we have thought of God as we have thought about some of those who raised us. Therefore, we have changed the loving face of God into a "superego- or conscience-oriented deity" who is looking over our shoulder, pointing out our deficits, and censuring us when we do something wrong. Few of us seem to live as adults before an "ego- or reality-oriented God" who loves us unconditionally in our ordinariness and wants us to be happy.

Unfortunately the distorted view we may have of God has been reinforced by the dry, dutiful pictures we often have been given of our relationship with the

Lord by religion. For instance, for many years when we looked into our catechisms for the answer to the question: "Why did God make you?" we probably found a very sterile and uninspiring answer that gave us a narrow, cold picture of our ideal relationship with the creator. One such common version I remember was: "To know, love, and serve God in this world and to be happy with him in the next."

Is this really why we were created by our living and loving God? Is this truly a vivid earthy reflection of that great lover Christ? Maybe it's time to recognize that we have confused the unconditional, warm, down-to-earth love of God with the conditional human caring of those who raised us. And perhaps we should take time to reflect instead on the following answer to the question of human creation found in one contemporary African catechism:

"Why did God make you?"

"Well, God thought you just might like it."[44]

Our real reflection today may then best be found in the accepting eyes of God. And so, if we can find a reflection in images of God that are loving and affirming of us as persons, we may then not only be able to have the solid self-esteem we should have as friends of God, but also be in a more secure position to correct those failings, self-perceptions, actions, and ways of living that go counter to our being created as the *imago Dei.*

The result would not only be better self-esteem and a healthy, free form of living our lives, but also an ability to be open to healthy criticism and to be a better friend to others. We would also be strong enough even to challenge societal and institutional (including the hierarchical church) structures when they oppress rather than enliven and empower all people.

The following story poetically illustrates the importance of one's self-image and the potentially powerful impact of having a good rather than distorted reflection of self. The message of this beautiful story reminds us of the basic themes of this chapter:

> The Iroquois Indians tell a fascinating story of a strange and unusual figure they call "the Peacemaker." The Peacemaker came to a village where the chief was known as "The Man-Who-Kills-and-Eats-People." Now the Man-Who-Kills-and-Eats-People, the chief, was in his wigwam. He had cut up his enemies and was cooking them in a massive pot in the center of the wigwam so that he might eat their flesh and absorb their mythical powers.
>
> The Peacemaker climbed to the top of the wigwam and looked down through the smokehole, say the Iroquois, and as he peered down through the smokehole his face was reflected in the grease

on the top of the pot. And the Man-Who-Kills-and-Eats-People looked into the pot, saw the reflection, and thought it to be his own face.

And, he said: "Look at that. That's not the face of a man who kills his enemies and eats them. Look at the nobility. Look at the peace in that face. If that is my face, what am I doing carrying on this kind of a life?"

And he seized the pot, dragged it from the fire, brought it outside and poured it out on the ground. He then called the people and said: "I shall never again take the life of an enemy. I shall never again destroy or consume an enemy for I have discovered my true face. I have found out who I am."

And then says the story, the Peacemaker came down from the top of the wigwam and embraced him and called him "Hiawatha."[45]

SELF-ESTEEM AND COMPASSION

From this story and the points made earlier, we can see that the way our self-image is formed can have a serious impact on our self-esteem (what we believe and how we feel about ourselves) and in turn affect how we lead our lives. If we are able to see our "true face" reflected in the loving eyes of God in prayer and in the faces of those who love us unconditionally, we ultimately then feel the confidence to see our own errors and shortcomings in a different way. Instead of viewing them as "proofs" that we are bad, we will see them as mistakes to be corrected or challenges to be taken on in life. The "positive paradox" is that with good self-esteem we will be in a better position to honestly examine our errors, addictions, pettiness, cowardice, greed, anger, and other failings. People with solid self-esteem don't measure their self-worth by how they perform. They are humble and know only God is perfect; in their enthusiasm they seek each day to receive the grace to be more responsive to what is good.

Given this, is it any wonder then that one of the most compassionate things we can actually do for others is to develop greater self-esteem ourselves? Or, in more colloquial terms, it makes sense that: One of the greatest things we can do for others is to learn to *like* ourselves, to "get a kick" out of ourselves!

The reason why having this type of attitude is actually helpful to others (rather than being merely narcissistic) is clear if we think about it. After all, people with solid self-esteem still feel the pain of rejection and failure but they are less defensive, better able to deal with the anxiety, stress, and negativity of others, and are in a better position to inspire true hope during difficult times. As Rollo May points out: "High self-esteem doesn't protect us from self-doubts but it does enable us to entertain self-doubts without being devastated." So, people with a good self-image can see difficult truths about themselves. They can withstand deserved and undeserved castigation by those whom they are trying to help, and still survive and learn from such interactions rather than be completely crushed by them.

People who know themselves and are at peace always have something to share—no matter how difficult the situation turns out to be. They are alive and those who encounter them enjoy the possibility of living more clear and meaningful lives because of the gentle space they can offer them. People who are in touch with their own gifts, and are grateful to God for them, seek to nurture these talents in themselves, and are in a fine position to be an emotional-spiritual oasis for the worried, poor, depressed, and oppressed of the world. They have let go of an over-concern with personal image. Their previously defensive energy has been freed up and converted into a creative source of strength which ultimately is made available for relationships with others in need. In essence, they are a place of true refuge.

As Louis Evely noted back in the 1960s:

> Since people don't have the courage to mature
> unless someone has faith in them, we have to
> reach those we meet at the level where they
> stopped developing, where they were given up on

as hopeless, and so withdrew into themselves and began to secrete a protective shell because they thought no one cared. They have to feel they're loved very deeply and very boldly before they dare appear humble, affectionate, sincere, and vulnerable.[46]

But following Evely's challenge to us to reach out to others, and knowing we are called to take our place in creation, a major question still remains for many of us: How can we do this for others if our own sense of self-esteem and self-respect is not really clearly present? Two important responses to this question are:

1. to respect ourselves as creations of God by cognitively appreciating (in the way we think, understand, and perceive) the awesome article of faith that we are made in the image and likeness of God. We do this by monitoring and vigorously confronting negative thinking about ourselves;

2. to affectively (emotionally) storm our "psyches" and hearts with images that reflect the belief that we are loved deeply by God through a process I would like to refer to here as "heartstorming."

In the remainder of this chapter we will first look at ways of confronting negative thinking. Following this we will focus on heartstorming.

BUILDING SELF-RESPECT

Enhancing one's self-respect is much more than an exercise in gaining greater personal comfort and security by improving one's image. It is nothing less than a psychological responsibility and a spiritual battle to accept the challenge to have greater sensitivity to the grandeur we have inherited, to be a living example for others who expect us to guide them, and to recognize that self-respect is a unique form of grateful worship to a God who has singled us out to be a reflection of divinity.

To know this deeply within oneself is to live differently. Yet, as one might suspect, this may mean at times that we must expend the necessary effort to recognize the unreasonable negative thoughts we sometimes have about ourselves, and to challenge such erroneous thinking with force and tenacity.

Self-respect is more than an ideal to wistfully think about. It is something to pray faithfully for each day and to act upon by reviewing the negative thoughts we may have about ourselves. There are many ways for us to inadvertently devalue ourselves as persons whether because of something we may have done, as a result of what people may be saying negatively about us, or because of some physical, psychological, intellectual, economical, or other lack real or imagined. When we vigorously oppose such thinking we are showing active respect for ourselves as creations of God.

The comedian Rodney Dangerfield made a living out of telling self-deprecating jokes about himself. For instance:

> When I was born, the doctor took one look at me and spanked my mother.

> When I was interested in dating, I sent a letter and a photo to the lonely-hearts club. They took one look at the photo and they said: "We're lonely . . . but not that lonely!

> As a result of all this rejection, I went to see a doctor about psychoanalysis. After taking one look at me, he told me to lie down on the couch—face down!

Aaron T. Beck, the founder of the cognitive-behavioral movement, likes to tell these stories to introduce his theory.[47] He believes that many of us attach meaning to a situation which results in our unnecessarily feeling badly about ourselves as persons. In Rodney Dangerfield's case, he took the statement "I am physically not as attractive as I would like to be," and changed it into the more drastic statement: "I am totally undesirable as a person."

Furthermore, as I have noted elsewhere:

> Negative thinking is quite common. For some reason, all of us seem to give more credence to the

negative than the positive. We can hear numerous positive things but somehow allow a few negative things to discolor and disqualify the previously affirming feedback we received. Therefore, we need to 1) pick up and recognize our negative thinking so we can 2) link the negative thoughts we have to the depressive/anxious feelings we experience, so 3) the negative self-talk we have can be replaced with a more realistic thought or belief. It is in this way that we structure changing our negative thinking so our negative beliefs can eventually be modified as well.

We can always—and, unfortunately, frequently do—find a negative comparison to make when we are reflecting on our thoughts, actions, and motivations. Therefore, when we do reflect and discern, our faith stance (which says we are loved and special) must be held onto firmly. Unless we grasp and embrace this reality, we will be drawn into making harmful comparisons which will neither help us to learn about ourselves nor aid us to discern the word of God in certain situations. Remember, finding something negative about ourselves is always easy. Making negative comparisons between our situations and those of others is never a problem. Maintaining perspective while we attempt to live simply in an anxious world is the difficulty![48]

Following the lead of Albert Ellis (a seminal thinker in the field of psychotherapy and founder of the Rational Emotive Therapy approach to treatment),[49] Beck also emphasizes the need to appreciate how we often personalize, "awfulize," mind-read, "catastrophize," and accept negative thoughts about ourselves without fully examining their veracity. As a result, Beck, Ellis, and people such as David Burns (the author of the very popular and useful self-help book *Feeling Good*) emphasize the need for greater sensitivity to how we think about ourselves. They encourage us to recognize typical negative reflections we have about ourselves during the day/week so we can examine and correct them. With respect to self-esteem they emphasize that since we think ourselves into problems by the way we value and respect ourselves, one of the best things we can and should do is to think ourselves out!

Such a psychological activity can be a helpful step to take in support of a spirituality which values all of creation—including, maybe especially, ourselves. For, once again, we are in a much better position to help others if we see the reflection of the sacred in ourselves ("Love your neighbor as yourself").

Given this, below is a brief list of principles (adapted from both the rational-emotive therapy and cognitive-behavioral schools of treatment) which simultaneously encourage self-respect and honesty about our failures. The process of altering inappropriate behavior can lead to a style of thinking which will increase self-esteem. In this mode one says, "I made a mistake. Naturally it is annoying and I feel somewhat bad about it. But it doesn't make me a bad person. What can I learn from it?" This is dramatically different from the negative mode which lowers self-esteem. In this mode one says, "I made this mistake; therefore I am a loser, no one likes me, and the people who criticize me are awful!"

PRINCIPLES OF SELF-RESPECT AND CLARITY

1. When I have made a mistake or feel anxious, I need to separate what I have done from who I am.

2. When I feel badly about myself as a person, I must see if I am embracing an irrational belief about myself. I need to take a distressful feeling as an opportunity to uncover a style of thinking and believing that undermines my self-respect or desire to understand and correct my behavior.

3. I must be sensitive to irrational thoughts and willing to challenge and dispute them. Thus I can affirm my self-respect and model it for those whom I wish to help. A common example of this is the irrational belief: "I must be perfect or

successful all of the time." This is ridiculous and impossible. It is based on such irrational beliefs as: if I make a mistake it undoes all that I've accomplished; it is all my fault; it means I am a terrible, unspiritual person; it will completely destroy my reputation in everyone's eyes; it cannot lead to anything good.

4. Since I am the one person I will have an intimate relationship with for my entire life, I need to take care of myself at least as well as I would care for others. Therefore, when I am feeling poorly about myself, I need to take steps to unconditionally accept myself and to help myself gain clarity and perspective in the same way as I would for someone else coming to me for empathy and support.

5. I need to be aware of depression producing, personally devaluing styles of thinking.[50] Some examples are:

   a. *Negative adding:* Because a few things have gone wrong I add them together and offer them to myself as "proof" that: I have a cloud over my head, "everything" is terrible in my life, I am a bad person, "a loser."

b. *Size distortion:* I magnify the unpleasant things that happen to me and minimize or dismiss the positive things.

c. *Negative contamination:* I allow one error, rejection, or unhappy instance to darken all my other accomplishments or positive attributes.

d. *"Awfulizing" or making myself upset or miserable:* I make an event into something horrible rather than seeing it as annoying, frustrating, or unfortunate.

e. *Being over-serious:* Rather than tease myself or exaggerate things until they are so ridiculous that I can laugh at them and myself, I actually believe that things are as bad as I think they are.

Much of what we accept as negative fact about ourselves is in reality lies. They are distortions which need to be uncovered for what they are rather than let stand. When we don't regularly challenge the distortions, negative thoughts, and beliefs we have about ourselves, they can remain as undetected "common nonsense" in our psyches or belief systems. They are like "psychological parasites" which quietly eat away at our self-esteem and self-respect. We need to recognize that it is not "the end of the world," "terribly sinful," or "catastrophic" if:

- Someone is angry with me;

- I make a mistake;

- Some people see some of my actions as failures;

- I don't work as hard at everything I do;

- I temporarily avoid some problem;

- Others are better at what they do than I am;

- Some people misunderstand my intentions or don't like me;

- Certain individuals don't take me seriously or may even laugh at me;

- Persons say negative things about me to my face or behind my back.

The above instances are merely annoyances. In fact, they are good opportunities to practice clear thinking as a means of supporting self-respect. We do this by stubbornly refusing to be overly upset about them, by seeking evidence for the belief that such situations are awful when they happen. When one cannot come up with enough evidence to really support that they are awful (and I am a terrible person), one seeks to develop alternate rational statements to replace the irrational ones that may have come to mind. For example, if someone says he doesn't like me and I feel bad for more than a reasonable amount of time, I should ask myself, "Why does this person's feelings about me mean I am undesirable as a person?" Then, recall that while this person may not like me, others do.

We need to recall that *all* religious figures, presidents, educators, business executives, philanthropists—no matter what their stature or giftedness—fail badly at times and are not accepted by everyone. As a matter of fact, since such leaders weren't prone to exaggerate the negative and become victims to self-devaluation or others' negative comments, they didn't withdraw from the intensity that comes with serious involvement with others, and actually increased their opportunities to help others and achieve positive societal goals.

Self-respect then is strengthened when we take the necessary time and energy to monitor our negative thoughts and evaluate our conclusions. This involves checking to see if we have unnecessarily exaggerated, minimized, or personalized negative thoughts in some way. Our self-respect grows when we recognize that we may have erroneously believed for years the fallacy that the negative deed makes the person bad.

God creates people with inherent value. So no mistake, failure, loss of image, exaggerated thinking, or hurtful comments by others can take this away or destroy this reality. We must stubbornly hold onto this fact of faith each day, for ourselves, for others, and in gratitude for being made in God's image. Because in "hating the sin, not the sinner" we will be in a position to embrace and learn from criticism without being crushed by it or hating the critic. And, in working hard at adopting this psychologically healthy way of thinking, we will be making an important spiritual statement of faith to ourselves and the world each day: "My identity and value come from being a creation of God . . . and from nowhere else!"

Images are in our heads, and the view we have of ourselves is already in our hearts. We need to ask: Is it the right self-image? In most cases, our anxieties, stresses, and depressive feelings tell us not quite. Well, what then is our true face? The use of creative positive imagery will certainly help us discover it.

CREATIVE POSITIVE IMAGERY

As has just been emphasized and illustrated, clear thinking is an essential cornerstone of self-respect. And so, the previous section reminded us that in the process of examining our actions and correcting our mistakes we must be careful not to cause ourselves unwarranted "narcissistic injury" (i.e., hurting the essence of who we are as persons). However, as crucial as cognitive clarity is, the spiritual life is more than a way of thinking. It is a way of living. And so, our journey to God must also involve the freedom to act justly on behalf of ourselves and others. And one of the best ways to support an attitude which is an outgrowth of sound self-esteem is through the constant creative use of imagery.

If we truly believe we are made in the image of God, we must develop a way of viewing ourselves that actually "feeds" this belief. The poet and Anglican divine Thomas Traherne put it beautifully when he noted back in the 1600s:

> You never enjoy the world aright till the sea itself floweth in your veins, till you are clothed with the heavens and crowned with the stars, and perceive yourself to be the sole heir of the whole world; and more so, because men are in it who are everyone sole heirs as well as you . . . till your spirit filleth the whole world, and the stars are your jewels, till you are familiar with the way of God in all ages as well as with your walk and table . . . till you delight in God for being good to all, you never enjoy the world.

Clear thinking helps us to uncover our irrational beliefs so we don't waste energy trying to please false gods (i.e., our image, extreme perfectionism, the need to be seen as unique or helpful) or be absorbed in negativity or trivialities. Imagery releases us to experience the vitality that is the result of our enthusiastic hearts meeting a welcoming, challenging, and enthusiastic God.

With imagery we are able to transform the question "What if?" into a sacramental experience because we are able to develop new resources within ourselves and to have a strong enough self-image to risk actions which in turn would further enhance a strong sense of self.

Too often our self-concept is poor:

> "Why is everyone here so happy except me?"
>
> "Because they have learned to see goodness and
>
> beauty everywhere" said the Master.
>
> "Why don't I see goodness and beauty everywhere?"
>
> "Because you cannot see outside of you what
> you fail to see inside."[51]

The reasons for a poor view of self are tied to some of the issues in self-esteem we have spoken about earlier. Our point here is that if low self-esteem can distort our images of self, then beautiful, strong, and gentle images can improve self-esteem.

In the spirit of Jesus' parable of the wheat and the chaff, Thich Nhat Hanh points out: "You don't need to directly encounter the seeds of your suffering; you can plant new seeds that have a healing nature. In other words, you can seed the unconscious."[52] Techniques that make creative use of imagery help us recognize, dispute, and replace our irrational beliefs with rational ones.

IN THE MIND'S EYE

Effective use of imagery can help us uncover new information, develop self-esteem, and prevent an erosion in our self-confidence. In his book, *In the Mind's Eye*, Arnold Lazarus point out:

> The use of imagery can often bypass verbal roadblocks and get to the root of the matter. Many people tend to over-intellectualize and they confuse everybody and themselves with verbiage. . . . *Find* the images and you will understand the behavior. Furthermore, find the images and, if you so desire, you will probably be able to *change* the feelings and the behavior.[53]

What most of us fail to realize is that we are using imagery all of the time without even being aware of it. For instance, if we image ourselves on the job as friendly and effective, the chances are we will smile, interact, and achieve more of what we set out to do than if we see ourselves as awkward and marginally talented. This does not mean that imagery can replace knowledge, but what it can do is to put that knowledge to work more effectively because if the script we are operating on has a good image of self as its basis, then the negative will be edited out and the positive emphasized.

As Matthew McKay and Patrick Fanning aptly point out in their helpful book *Self-Esteem*:

> You can replace much of [the] negative propaganda with [new] visualized scenes. Consider visualization as a method for reprogramming the way you make simple decisions. Every instant of every day you are faced with tiny, mostly unconscious decisions. Should you turn right or left? Have toast or a muffin?
>
> Visualization reprograms your mind to recognize and choose the slightly more positive of any two choices. Over time, the sum of thousands of tiny positive choices is higher self-esteem and a lot more happiness.
>
> This programming of your automatic decision making is nothing new. You do it already, but if you have low self-esteem, you do it in reverse. You visualize and subsequently choose the negative path. . . . You gravitate toward the negative people, the painful situations. . . . You can use [visualization then] to change all this. You can use it to give a conscious positive nudge to what has heretofore been an automatic, subconscious, and negative process.[54]

IMAGERY EXERCISES

Two imagery enhancement exercises help us practice using imagery in a basic way to improve the skill of visualization and to increase our ability in observing reality more clearly and accurately.[55] They are easy, fun, and take only a few minutes.

EXERCISE 1 — OBJECT RECALL

Object recall is an exercise that helps us to be more observant and improve basic imagery skills. Simply look at an object, close your eyes, and try to recall it. Bring to mind the size, color, texture, and shape. Bring it into sharp focus in your mind. Then open your eyes and see how close you came to visualizing it. Do it a second time, but this time try to increase your accuracy. After opening your eyes and seeing how well you did, repeat the exercise with another object. By doing this several times a day for a few weeks, your imagery skill will improve.

EXERCISE 2 — IMAGE MANIPULATION

Another exercise that is helpful and enjoyable is to picture a bare bulb hanging in an empty room. Then in your mind's eye make it dim. Following this slowly make it brighter and brighter until it is glaring. Following this change bring the luminescence down until you can look at the bulb without squinting and change the color into a cool green. Let the green fill the room with a sense of coolness. Then change the color to orange and make it get very, very bright until it makes the whole room look like the inside of a halloween lantern. The four walls of the room should have a glowing orange hue to them. Then change the light to a soft pink and make it so dim that the room has a light Bermuda hue to it. And finally change it to a bright red, making it brighter and brighter until the room almost feels hot. Change it back at last to white and then open your eyes.

These two basic exercises have a number of variations. They show us that we do have images in our mind and can bring them to consciousness and change them if we wish. Doing them also sets the stage for a daily exercise on developing spiritual self-esteem that I would like to refer to as "heartstorming." In this simple exercise, a little preparation is called for but the effort is worth it because it can then be used each day. It also can be updated as time goes on and we grow in self-knowledge.

HEARTSTORMING

1. The first preparatory step is to write down what you feel your God-given talents are, ones that you are grateful for, ones that are a joy to have and to share.

2. Next, ask some trusted friends to share with you what they like about you and feel are your gifts. If you feel awkward asking, you can phrase the question like this: "I feel like I bury some of my gifts, ignore others, and am not even aware of still others; I would like to prize them, be grateful for them each day, and do what I can to share them with others. I feel a bit self-conscious asking you this but your views would help. What do you see as my God-given gifts?"

3. When this list is as complete as you can make it, take the third preparatory step: try to see if your list has an overriding theme to it. Can it be distilled to a single word or name? For example, people may feel you are very enabling and enthusiastic, or that you have a deep sense of vitality. Is "vitality" your word? Or do people see you as quiet, patient, a listener, someone who offers them a sense of presence? Is "presence" your word, your "name," if you will, in your own and your friends' eyes?

4. At this point, we can take an additional step by looking through scripture for a figure who we feel has a name similar to ours. For instance, if we feel we are very outgoing, gregarious, and inspirational, if we have a deep sense of vitality that we like to share with others through motivation and exhortation, we might find the apostle Paul to be our role

model. Doing this is helpful because it not only gives us a concrete individual to emulate, but also encourages us to search out scripture more closely. We might want to find out about this person, or we might want to see if another character in scripture would be even more appropriate as a role model. This process is especially exciting for women today since we now have more scholarship available on feminist interpretations of scripture.

Once we have a list of positive talents, a theme, if possible, a one-word name for our central charism, and a scriptural figure for a role model, then we can proceed to the simple exercise of heartstorming.

1. The first step is to find a quiet place of solitude (you can even do it in bed just before rising in the morning or in the shower if silence and solitude are at a premium).

2. The second basic step is to try to relax yourself. Just breathe deeply and steadily. Notice any tightness in your body as you do this. Relax any tight part of your face, neck, chest, arms, stomach, buttocks/ pelvic area, thighs, calves, and feet as you exhale. Although there are more extensive approaches to relaxation, this simple method will suffice as a starting point.

3. Once relaxed, the third basic step is to image yourself as the person who has this word, this "name" you have found for yourself. Picture yourself meeting people and doing things during the day as someone who really has embraced this style of interacting with others. For instance, if your word is "vitality," picture yourself being enthusiastic and supportive. You might envision yourself as Paul the apostle, working hard to encourage others even in the face of difficulties. The sky's the limit to this phrase of the exercise: only your own imagination determines the boundaries. That is why some practice to develop the imagination is helpful.

You can do this exercise for as long as you like. The exercise can be extended by picturing yourself interacting with more and more people in a greater variety of situations. If at any point you get distracted by a person or situation in your imagination and start to feel angry, anxious, or negative in some way, go back and rest in the word you chose for yourself. Picture God standing next to you smiling in encouragement. You can then picture yourself with poise and return to the exercise.

4. The next step is to recall your word during the day and to take small steps in which you "act" as if you completely owned this "name." The important thing to remember at this stage is not to pick on

yourself if you fall short in some way. You must remember the apostle Paul kept wondering why he would fail at times (Rom 7:17). But he also knew and reminded himself that the gift of God's grace would see him through. As Jesus reminded us: "With God all things are possible" (Mk 10:27, KJV).

The power of imagery is amazing, if only we use it. In addition to the brief introduction offered above, many books specifically on the topic of imagery treat this issue much more extensively than can be done here and offer additional exercises for the imagination.

SELF-ESTEEM AND THE SPIRITUAL JOURNEY

Anthony A. Hoekema, a former professor of systematic theology at Calvin Theological Seminary in Grand Rapids, Michigan, once wrote: "The Christian life does not merely involve believing something about Christ; it also involves believing something about ourselves. Having a proper Christian self-image, therefore, is an aspect of our Christian faith. Conversely, failing to see ourselves as new creatures in Christ is a denial of our faith."[56]

In saying this, Professor Hoekema was not denying sin or that Christians do things that are wrong. Instead he was echoing a theme of one his former professors Henry Schultze who said: "You cannot think too seriously about your sins, but you can think too exclusively about them."[57] For instance, with respect to the apostle Paul, Professor Hoekema notes:

> Paul often saw himself as a great sinner. He never described himself as a sinner, however, without at the same time referring to the grace of God, which forgave his sins, accepted him, and enabled him to be useful in God's kingdom. . . . Paul in other words exemplified the attitude of believers, who without minimizing [their] sins, refuse to be constantly hypnotized by them.[58]

Maybe we are hypnotized by our sins because we are more fearful of the alternative: that we really are the *imago Dei*. What would happen if we intercepted our negative feelings, connected them with our negative thinking, and disputed our cognitive distortions with more correct positive thinking? What would happen if we replaced outmoded images of God and ourselves with positive, challenging ones that would call us to take our place in the kingdom? Would we have peace? Would we be happy?

I think sometimes, without knowing it, we fear emotional and spiritual passion more than we seem to fear our rigidity and lack of courage. We fear unconditional love more than rejection. We fear the newness of the gospel, the good news, more than we fear being mired in attitudes and beliefs that have us frozen in the present way we view everything. As I mentioned previously the paradox is that we complain the most about our lack of spiritual passion when we are willing to risk the least.

Pat McCloskey notes:

> Often we drag along behind us images of God—and related images of ourselves and others—that are increasingly heavy. Yet we refuse to leave them behind because we fear that new images might be even heavier in the sense of requiring an even greater conversion on our part. Try as they may, other people can only challenge our images, point out self-contradictions, and encourage us to convert, to discover more adequate, more generous, more truthful images about all three. No one else can cut the rope that binds us to images we do not fully trust yet are unwilling to leave behind. The images of God we may be dragging around with great weariness are the same images that, whether we intend it or not, we are conveying to others.[59]

But with courage, with trust, with grace, maybe we can risk thinking clearly and imaging God and ourselves boldly and dramatically. Maybe we can clear our minds of unnecessary negativity and storm our hearts with appropriate biblical images of hope. When we do this, the challenges we are anxious about may still appear—but along with them the peace and excitement that come with really risking to live the spiritual life will also overtake, cradle, and warm us! This will turn out not only to be exhilarating for us, but it will also be a guiding light for others who wish to seek a deep vitality for themselves but are too afraid because of past hurts and failures.

If anything then, solid self-esteem based on God's love for us in our ordinariness offers us a real chance to live nobly and honorably and to help others along the way. Living any other way, with a view of self that is any less than God's view of us, God who wrote our names on the palms of his hands (Is 49:16), is unnecessarily tragic and sad. If we can remember this each day—no matter how we feel or what is facing us—we can then be as spiritually audacious as God has intended us to be all along. And that would be just wonderful, wouldn't it?

Part Three

FRIENDSHIP

Four

FRIENDS

*T*he beauty of ordinariness is revealed, supported, and enhanced by the presence of good friends. In his helpful book, *Making All Things New*, Henri Nouwen notes that: "We can take a lot of physical and even mental pain when we know that it truly makes us a part of the life we live together in the world. But when we feel cut off from the human family, we quickly lose heart."[60] I think this is true. Reflection on my own life and the work I have done with persons experiencing emotional stress, spiritual hunger, and personal alienation seems to bear this out.

This point becomes even more relevant when we realize that although for most of early adulthood we seem to have a ready-made community, after that, things often change dramatically. The demands of our particular vocation and the needs of those who depend on us take center stage. What we can accomplish as individuals seems to become more important at the very time our community of friends becomes less present to us.

A good example of a group of persons who experience this problem is the clergy. In seminary or divinity school there is a rich mixture of friends to interact with an daily basis and a schedule or structure that encourages interaction with them, no matter how busy things get. Then, following ordination, the cleric moves out into the parish, into a turbulent sea of needs and demands which require a good deal of attention and time. And even if there is a pastor present with whom one will serve, the concern about "performing well" decreases rather than enhances the possibility of a friendship of equals and of mutual support.

Viewing this issue from a broader perspective, we can readily see that although this may be a particular problem for the clergy, it is obviously by no means reserved to them. Most adults have to face this challenge. This is a shame particularly because friends are not only important for support, but are also necessary for psychological and spiritual growth—if you will, for holiness.

That is why books, lectures, and counselors stress the need to see a special value in establishing, maintaining, and further developing a more balanced community of friends. Trying to mature psychologically through sheer effort or through individualistic forms of piety tends to spell disaster. Recognition of the fact that we need good friends to encourage us to greater personal depth and openness is only a first, albeit important, step. One of the practical and difficult questions that still remains to be answered is: What *types* of friends do I need to have a healthy and challenging community?

Even in the best of interpersonal times, the mix of friends we have varies. That is, of course, natural. Surprisingly, it may not be as relevant as it might seem at first blush. Instead, I think that the important factor is whether there are people in our lives whom we can trust and who are able to play a number of different crucial roles. Four of them that I would like to present here are: "prophet," "cheerleader," "harasser," and "spiritual guide."

Without all of these voices in our community, we run the risk that our experiences and perceptions will be too limited, and that this will be reflected in our emotional and spiritual life. When one tries to live a committed life that is devoid of rich community, extreme and prolonged degrees of negative feelings can result. One experiences such feelings as boredom, apathy, loneliness, burnout, righteousness, anger, restlessness, depression, moodiness, ambivalence, and anxiety.

Even though negative emotions such as these are usually correctly attributed to social, financial, physical, and psychological causes, they often have a spiritual side as well. As a matter of fact, although the cause and symptoms may be varied, the primary source may in fact be spiritual in nature. In many instances, emotional disturbances occur because we have put our psychological and spiritual hands around something or someone less than God's will.

At points like this, the good thing about a rich mixture of friends is that they can help us improve our sense of psychological perspective and can further engender spiritual single-heartedness. Whether it be in confusing, painful, joyful, or even comfortable (possibly idolatrous) times, friends can reach out—each in different ways—to help us find "the way" when we are temporarily lost. In addition, they can assist us to better appreciate ourselves when we seem to be haunted by self-doubt and help us to open up new opportunities to meet God in surprising ways.

THE PROPHET

Sometimes one friend is able to play multiple roles in our life, and for that reason I will call these roles "voices." The first of these voices which help us maintain balance and have a sense of openness is the one I shall refer to as the prophet. Contrary to what one might imagine, prophetic friends need not look or behave any differently than other types of persons who are close to us. In reality, prophets only occasionally present themselves like John the Baptist: wild, woolly, and obvious. In many cases people who do come across that way are not the real prophets; they are far from being "characters of God" who, instead of merely talking about truth, are actual bearers and living models of the Spirit.

False prophets often come across in a convincingly dramatic way. I do not doubt that they have had a special encounter with God at one or more points in their lives. But somewhere along the way they have made a crucial error, one that we can all learn from. They have forgotten the place of grace in their own lives and are consequently taking themselves, instead of God, very seriously. Due to this, their personalities are projecting themselves so loudly that they can't hear the quiet prophetic voice guiding their own behavior. Thus they are in no position to help others in need.

The true prophet's voice is often quiet and fleeting, but nonetheless strong. She or he is living an honest and courageous life guided by truth and compassion. With the grace of God they are trying to live out the truth, and whether knowingly or not, they follow the advice of Gandhi: "Let our first act every morning be this resolve: I shall not fear anyone on earth. I shall fear only God. I shall not bear ill-will toward anyone. I shall conquer untruth by truth and in resisting untruth, I shall put up with all suffering."

The message of prophets often involves discomfort or pain, not masochistic pain, but real pain. Often they do not directly produce conflict. Instead, like leaders in the nonviolent movement, they "merely" set the stage for it, as is pointed out in the following words of Martin Luther King, Jr.:

> We who engage in nonviolent, direct action are not the creators of tension. We merely bring to the surface the hidden tension that is already alive. We bring it out in the open, where it can be seen and dealt with. Like a boil that can never be cured so long as it is covered up but must be opened with all its ugliness to the natural medicines of air and light, injustice must be exposed, with all the tension its exposure creates, to the light of human conscience and the air of national opinion before it can be cured.

Having someone prophetic in our lives is never easy. No matter how positive we may believe the ultimate consequences will be for us, many of us still shy away from prophetic messages and would readily agree with Henry Thoreau: "If you see someone coming to do you a good deed, run for your life!" However, to seek comfort in lieu of the truth may mean that in an effort to avoid pain, we will also avoid responding to opportunities of real value, real life. We will merely exist and eventually die without having every really lived.

As Allen Boesak of South Africa says: "We will go before God to be judged, and God will ask us: 'Where are your wounds?' And we will say, 'We have no wounds.' And God will ask, 'Was nothing worth fighting for?'" I wonder if we wouldn't feel justified in responding to Boesak: "Oh, I don't have to worry about that challenge. Look at all my wounds!" But I think many of our so-called wounds result from a lack of faith and trust in the Lord. We desire to fill our arms with our own-fashioned crosses rather than leave them open for the crosses God might wish us to bear.

Seen in this light then, the crosses we bear much of the time are the direct result of our being primarily concerned with something or someone other than God. Even though we believe a lot of the pain we experience is due to our involvement in life and the direct result of reaching out to others (which is sometimes true), it is actually more often than not the product of our putting faith in someone or something less than God. In such instances our worries, insecurities, and preoccupations are due to a lack of faith and a desire to hold onto, or have returned to us, a particular status quo.

For example, we may believe we can only feel secure and happy if our adolescent son behaves as we want, if our elderly parent stays healthy forever, if our friends appreciate us more, or if the institutional church follows our ideas now. Instead, while such occurrences might be helpful from our point of view, in the spirit of the words and ministry of Jesus, true peace will not be produced by getting what we want in every situation. It can only result from placing primary value on what we believe God wants of us (obedience), being in true solidarity with others in life (community), and doing everything in a spirit of love (the greatest law of life).

I think Sheila Cassidy (a physician who was tortured in Chile for treating a revolutionary) points to the heart of the matter when she notes: "If we can come to want only what God wants, then we are in a curious way untouchable; for then loss of property, of good name, or health, or even of life holds no fear, for if that is what God wants, we will be at peace." It is at this point that theonomy (God's rule) equals autonomy (our rule). At a juncture such as this we become truly free.

Still, what would we do if we really believed this? What if we got up tomorrow morning and could truly forgive others and feel deeply forgiven by God? What if, in the spirit of the ammas and abbas of the African desert, we were able to begin each day afresh without worry or agendas? What would we do as an encore? If we didn't fill our hearts and heads with worry, the desire to control, or addictions, but "simply" enjoyed what was before us and found God there, what would we have to complain about most of the time? How would we live an undistracted life which would force us to then face the angst of our own limitedness, help-lessness, lies, and our own eventual death? These are the questions with which prophets help us.

Prophets point! They point to the fact that it doesn't matter whether pleasure or pain is involved, the only thing that matters is that we seek to be with God in what we do and how we think, feel, and image our-selves and the world. In other words that we seek to see and live "the truth" because only it will set us free.

In doing this, prophets challenge us to look at how we are living our lives, to ask ourselves: "To what voices am I listening when I form my attitudes and take my actions each day?" For instance, I think there is an overwhelming glut of negativity in the media that says: "All is lost." As a result, evil often manifests itself as "sensible despair." The evil of omission is not actually the failure to do impressive things for each other and God. When faced with obstacles to doing the great things and overcoming the great evils which we have deemed important, we may give way to a despair. This is the evil of omission that prevents us from doing the little things that we could do, the small things God may be calling us to do.

Paradoxically, appreciating the presence of great problems in the world can seem to remove our responsibility to act in good faith rather than serve to call us to a more faithful sense of commitment at a time when the world truly needs us. We forget that doing what we can is a true countercultural act of faith, especially when surrounded by voices that say: "Don't bother. All is lost; no matter what you do, you can't make a difference."

The following little story may illustrate this theme more clearly. As you read it picture the sparrow in it as the committed spiritual person and the horseman as "secularism."

> It was a chilly, overcast day when the horseman spied the little sparrow lying on its back in the middle of the road. Reining in his mount, he looked down and inquired of the fragile creature: "Why are you lying upside down like that?"
>
> The sparrow replied: "Oh, early this morning I heard that the sky is going to fall later today."
>
> Upon hearing this, the horseman laughed derisively and said: "And I suppose your spindly legs can hold up the heavens?"
>
> To which the sparrow replied: "One does what one can."[61]

The question prophets present to us is: Are we still doing what we can? And their confrontations with us point out how much more we need to do things in a loving way that allows the world to see the face of God in our actions. They want us to respond to the challenge Neitzsche made to Christians many years ago. It is unfortunately still a quite valid challenge today. He said: "I will never believe in the Christian redeemer until Christians show me that they themselves have been redeemed."

THE CHEERLEADER

Ironically, one of the most controversial suggestions I might make with respect to friendship is to suggest we all need "cheerleaders." To suggest we need people to be prophetic in our lives is readily understandable. We can all see how easy it is to lose our way in our desire to control our own destinies, be secure, deny our death, and insulate ourselves from God's call "to act justly, to love tenderly and to walk humbly with your God" (Mi 6:8, JB). But to say that we need "cheerleaders" is quite a different matter!

Some might say that to encourage this type of friend is to run the risk of narcissism and denial. However, to balance the prophetic voices and to let us see the reflection of the loving face of God more readily in the world, we also need unabashed, enthusiastic, unconditional acceptance by certain people in our lives.

Prophecy can and should instill appropriate guilt to break through the crusts of our denial. But guilt cannot sustain us for long. While guilt will push us to do good things because they are right, love encourages us to do the right thing because it is natural.

When we are in pain, the first person to turn to is not the prophet. At times like this we need loving support so we don't lose total perspective in the situation. So, at the end of a discouraging hurtful day, when we call supportive friends of the type being suggested here, they can hold us in their hearts and help us remember we are loved and loveable.

In my book *Seeking Perspective* I tease people:

> [We all] need the kind of individuals who in response to our complaints about others, give us so much support that we almost feel guilty. And when we express some annoyance at a person or persons, they say something to the effect: "You are totally right and they are totally wrong. As a matter of fact, I am getting on my knees this very moment to pray for their early happy death!"[62]

Behind my silly musings there is a serious point that deserves emphasis. We can't go it alone. We need a balance of support. We need encouragement and acceptance as much as we need the criticism and feedback that are difficult to hear. Burnout is always around the corner when we don't have people who are ready to encourage us, see our gifts clearly, and be there for us when our involvement with people, their sometimes unrealistic demands, and our own crazy expectations for ourselves threaten to pull us down.

I do recognize that to have the "cheerleader" without the prophet may lead to projecting the blame for everything on others and becoming too self-righteous to recognize and admit one's own mistakes. And I grant this would be a very dangerous situation. Yet, to have our lives filled with prophecy without the presence of God's mercy and love as it is reflected in friends who get joy out of seeing the footprints of God in our personality, is to set the stage for skepticism, sarcasm, defeatism, and despair. Such attitudes cannot help but lead us away from religious and social involvement because one is so emotionally and spiritually tired that there seems to be no energy left to continue.

Another problem that supportive people in our community of friends help us to deal with is the presence of the "deadly gnats" that plague when we are trying to help others. The angry, hyper-sensitive, passive-aggressive, and overall needy behavior of one or more people whom we serve, with whom we work, or who are supposed to be supporting us, is understandable. So many people, having come from dysfunctional families, seem burdened with problems today. However, even though this is the case, having to continually absorb the negativity or demanding behavior of others can be a slow and almost indiscernible drain on our energy that leads to disastrous results if left unchecked.

A number of years ago a large search was undertaken for a chancellor for a major university system. After a long and arduous process, he was chosen, only to have him resign after less than a year in office. When asked about this, he said that it wasn't anything major that was overwhelming. It was the "gnats" that got to him. The constant bickering, complaints, obstructions, minor hostilities, hyper-sensitivity, and other such stresses sapped his energy and made him feel overwhelmed, under-appreciated, and drained of creativity.

I didn't fully understand his situation until it happened to me a number of years ago. I was scheduled to go to Canada to lead a series of workshops for a group of teachers who were undergoing a great deal of stress. Just before leaving, I made a mistake in how I handled something at work. In response to this, one of the persons who worked with me unleashed various levels of anger. Open sarcasm, negative comments to others, and a disrespectful personal memo. (I'm sure practically everyone has received this type of message at one time or another—one with an exclamation point after a decisive comment about one's inability to handle something correctly.)

I knew this episode bothered me even though I tried to handle it with a sense of calm and poise. I finally realized the full impact of it on the morning of the first workshop I was to lead. Upon waking, I rose, sat on the edge of my bed, and discovered I felt beaten and upset. I thought to myself: "My heart is so tired; how will I ever be able to reach out to those counting on me today?"

I could see that I set up my very active schedule with the unrealistic expectation that I would never run into problems with the people who were hired to support my efforts. I also had conveniently forgotten the difficulty I normally have in dealing with people's anger and the problem I still have with overconcern about my own image. (These things always serve to remind me of my continued need for God's grace and greater humility.)

Later that morning, I was thankful that when I saw the faces of the teachers with whom I was to work, I did get energized by their deep sense of commitment and was then able to respond competently and from the heart with a sense of honesty.

I knew the issue was not resolved and when I got home I shared the episode with my wife. I explained why I felt the person who was so angry with me touched a sensitive chord. I mentioned that if I had another job opportunity, I might be tempted to commit the "sin" of taking it even though I still felt called to be in my current position; I just felt like running away from a situation where instead of support, I was feeling the pain of little knives in my back. I was also feeling sorry for myself and kept thinking: "Where do people get the time and energy to be such a pain?"

Her response was: "You know you are a good person and yet you are giving away too much power to those who are angry with you. It's not fair to you or to those who count on you. You may have made a mistake in judgment but you didn't deserve the amount of anger and certainly not the disrespect you received as a result. A responsible adult should have given you the benefit of the doubt or at the very least come to speak with you about his sense of hurt instead of behaving as an angry two-year-old. Try to recognize though that the person with whom you are dealing may not even realize he is acting out inappropriately. It may be necessary to ensure a more formal style of relationship between the two of you and to confront him on his lack of respect should he act that way in the future. But also recognize that he may not understand. After all, aren't you always advising people to have low expectations and high hopes when dealing with others?"

Her comments were just what I needed to hear to help me regain necessary perspective and feel appropriate self-love. She helped me to encounter the love of God during a very difficult time for me. With her support I could once again agree with W.S. Gilbert's comment: "You have no idea what a poor opinion I have of myself, and how little I deserve it!"

So, while having buoyantly supportive friends may seem like a luxury, make no mistake about it—it is a necessity that is not to be taken lightly. The "interpersonal roads" of time are strewn with well-meaning helpers who tried to survive without such support. Encouragement is a gift that should be treasured in today's stressful, anxious, complex world because the seeds of involvement and the seeds of burnout are the same. To be involved is to risk. And to risk without the presence of solidly supportive friends is foolhardy and dangerous. Warm friends represent the incarnational love of God in our lives and remind us, in the words of Paul Tillich, that faith is best defined as "the courage to accept acceptance."

THE HARASSER

Along with the prophet and cheerleader, another essential type of friend is the "harasser." This type of friend can help us to face a danger that everyone trying to be committed to God risks: on the way to taking God seriously, we may end up taking ourselves too seriously instead.

When singer-activist Joan Baez was asked her opinion about Thomas Merton, one of the things she said was that he was different than many of the phony gurus she had encountered in her travels. She said that although Merton took important things seriously in his life, he didn't take himself too seriously. She indicated that he knew how to laugh at situations and particularly at himself.

In many instances, we fail to be like a Merton and we lose perspective because of it. A number of years ago I gave a lecture to a particular group of undergraduates and it went terribly instantly. To make matters worse, when I become anxious in such situations, I tend to speed up. So, even though I just started teaching the course, by the end of the class period I felt I had already finished presenting the main points of my entire semester's notes!

After the class was over, I stepped out into the hall feeling awful. One of my colleagues, who is also a psychologist and happened to be standing at the end of the hallway, saw my face, and was at my side in an instant. (Because you know how they love to treat their own!)

He said to me: "You look depressed. Why is that?"

"I just gave a presentation and it went terribly from the beginning; it was like a rock in water."

"But why are you depressed?" he repeated.

"They were so bored that they continually checked their watches to see if their batteries were running!"

Again he asked: "But why are you depressed?"

"I couldn't believe how disinterested they were; they did something that I didn't think was anatomically possible—they actually yawned in unison!"

He steadfastly asked again: "But why are you depressed?"

By then I was not only depressed but also furious at him: "After all I have told you, why shouldn't I be depressed?"

"Because five seconds after you left the room, they probably forgot what your name was."

To this I exclaimed while laughing: "My goodness! Isn't there any easier way we could put this in perspective?"

Obviously this story points out how I was guilty of the sin of "negative grandiosity." I was taking myself so seriously that I was pulling myself down. "Harassers" help us to laugh at ourselves and to avoid the emotional burnout resulting from having the unrealistic expectation that people will always follow our guidance or appreciate what we do for them. This type of friend helps us regain and maintain perspective (so we don't unnecessarily waste valuable energy). This is truly a gift for which we can be thankful.

SPIRITUAL GUIDES

The three types of friends we've looked at thus far are each part of a necessary community. The prophet enhances our sense of single-heartedness. The cheerleader generously showers us with the support we feel we need. The harasser encourages us to maintain a sense of proper perspective. Complementing these three is a cluster that, for lack of a better name, shall be referred to as "spiritual guides."

Recently I was invited to Denver to help celebrate the inauguration of a new program in pastoral counseling. My attention was piqued when I overheard a member of a Catholic religious community speak about one of her sisters who went to Denver many, many years ago to ask for material support.

The woman religious about which the story was being told was dressed in the full religious habit of the day and appeared at the fence of a farm outside the city limits of Denver. After she had been standing there for a period of time the man who owned the farm spotted her. He walked down to meet her and asked if he could be of help. She blurted out: "I wonder if you could donate a cow to my community?"

Not being Catholic, he didn't know what to make of the request. But after pausing to scratch his head and reflect for a moment, he smiled, shrugged, and said: "Why not?"

After hearing this reply and realizing that she hadn't even told the generous farmer anything about her congregation's work before asking for his help, she quickly added: "You know, we have been begging for help for over one hundred years." He retorted with a laugh: "Gee, you'd think by now that you'd have all you need."

When I recall this enjoyable story, I feel a similar sentiment about myself and my own journey in life. My thought is: "You would think by now, I would have enough of the information and experience I need in order to live a good and vital spiritual life." However, as we all realize, it is not as easy as that. We will never cease to need an array of spiritual guides to help us deal with our *unrecognized and unnecessary fears*, to help us to appreciate the need for proper *detachment*, and to lead us to a sense of *enthusiasm and perspective* in a world strained by anxiety and confusion.

FEAR

Fear can be very dangerous. A book published in 1989 on negativity indicated that fear can lead to an unhealthy desire for withdrawal. In this book, the authors note: "Because people are afraid of fear, they give up acre after acre of their own life. Some find the snapping of twigs so uncomfortable that they abandon the territory of life entirely."[63] At the other extreme, as Bertrand Russell aptly points out, fear can lead to aggression: "Fear is the main source of superstition, and one of the main sources of cruelty. To conquer fear is the beginning of wisdom."

A major role of spiritual guides is to help us discover our fears. They help us ask ourselves: What is the *worst* thing that can happen if we face our fears? One of the greatest hidden fears is the anxiety we have when we forget God's unconditional love. When this happens, we waste a great deal of energy being preoccupied with what will happen if the image we wish to project to the world does not come across.

Too often we invest an inordinate amount of energy trying to be seen as someone who is hardworking, helpful, successful, unique, knowing, loyal, nice, powerful, or acceptable. In such instances, we hold onto the erroneous belief that we must hide, at all cost, our anger, pride, deceit, envy, stinginess, fear, self-indulgence, arrogance, or laziness. We hide behind a screen of efforts that "prove" (to ourselves, others, and God) that we are perfect.

In such cases our fears are not real. They are actually unnecessary anxieties that come from failing to believe that our ordinariness is all that matters in the eyes of God. We attempt to build up an image in our own and others' eyes because we lack the trust to believe that in God's eyes being simply ourselves (ordinary) is enough. To make matters worse, our response to this lack of faith is often manifested in actions that demonstrate a willful desire to go it alone, to be independent of the creator or to deny the need for grace. Rabbi Abraham Heschel describes this process poetically:

> After having eaten the forbidden fruit, the Lord sent forth man from paradise, to till the ground from which he was taken. But man, who is more subtle than any other creature that God has made, what did he do? He undertook to build a paradise by his own might, and he is driving God from his paradise.[64]

And so, our guides listen to us carefully and don't accept the "manifest content" (what we say and do) as being equal to the "total content" (our actual intentions plus our statements and actions). Instead, they search and look for nuances in what we share with them to help us to uncover some of the "voices" that are unconsciously guiding our lives, especially the ones that undermine our trust in God and make us hesitant, anxious, fearful, and willful.

DETACHMENT

Simone Weil once said that "Attachment is the great fabricator of illusions; reality can be attained only by someone who is detached." But the subject of detachment is not an easy one to appreciate. Possibly the best way of illustrating the principle is to look at the problem of inordinate attachment as it is reflected in the following story about the proper way to catch monkeys.

Since monkeys are very bright and frenetic, they are difficult to catch without causing them harm. So some people have devised a simple technique to capture them. They empty out gourds, fill them with peanuts, and then patch up the gourds so only a small opening remains in each one. They then attach the gourds to trees and leave the area.

After a while, when the monkeys feel safe and all is quiet, they come down from the trees, stick their hands in the gourds and grab a handful of peanuts. However, once they do this, they can not get their hands out of the gourds.

To escape, all they need do is let go of the peanuts. But they hold on, screaming with fear and frustration. Finally the trappers come back and catch them.[65]

The question spiritual guides present us with is: What peanuts are we holding onto that are preventing us from experiencing God's peace? As Jesus noted: "Wherever your treasure is, there will your heart be too" (Mt 6:21). What preoccupies and troubles us most of the time (what we think about the first thing in the morning, what concerns us as we drive or walk around during the day, and what we think about shortly before going to bed)? Most often, these are our "peanuts," our "gods." Spiritual guides teach us proper discernment with respect to those people and things in our lives that we love.

In keeping with the following excerpt from Jewish spiritual wisdom, spiritual guides first encourage us to fully enjoy our family, friends, success, food, money, health—all the gifts of God.

> The Jerusalem Talmud states that when, after life, one will confront ultimate judgement, one of the issues on the table will be whether one denied oneself the experience of those enjoyments that God had made available, and if so, why? God does not play games, making enjoyable pleasures available, but then saying you cannot touch them, you cannot enjoy them. On the contrary, by denying, one misses the experience of God's majesty.[66]

However, they also subsequently point out that when we have become so attached to these gifts that we are no longer disciplined in their use and feel we cannot be happy without them, then we are not free anymore. Then something is wrong.

The apostles who experiences the transfiguration were obviously not expected to close their eyes to the beauty of the experience. (To do so would be to fool-ishly turn their backs on a wonderful gift of God; more than that, it would be an act of ingratitude.) But, on the other hand, neither were they then called to "set up tents" there. Instead, they were expected—through this experience of God—to be free to carry the experi-ence within them and go out into the unknown future, even to Jerusalem. So, from all of this, the question we are asked to grapple with by our spiritual guides today is: Are we both truly grateful for the people and things God has given us to enjoy in our lives, but also willing to let go of them rather than to try to hold onto, control, or idolize them?

The following story aptly summarizes this theme. As members of an efficient, frequently insecure con-temporary society it is so difficult for us to accept the wisdom of the desert:

> Abba Doulas, the disciple of Abba Bessarion, said: "When we were walking along the sea one day, I was thirsty, so I said to Abba Bessa-rion, 'Abba, I am very thirsty.' Then the old man prayed, and said to me, 'Drink from the sea.' The water was sweet when I drank it. And I poured it into a flask, so that I would not be thirsty later.

Seeing this, the old man asked me, 'Why are you doing that?' I answered, 'Excuse me, but it's so that I won't be thirsty later on.' Then the old man said, 'God is here, and God is everywhere.'"[67]

ENTHUSIASM AND PERSPECTIVE

Spiritual guides also seek out the true inner charism in people (cf. 1 Cor 12). Our gifts are like sparks that need to be fanned into a flame, not put under a bushel basket. They have been given to us by God to share with others in a spirit of enthusiasm and perspective. To accomplish this, spiritual guides must continually help people discern the distinction between genuine enthusiasm and other emotions that merely mimic it.

For instance, enthusiasm and exhilaration are not the same thing. Exhilaration may be present when we are enthusiastic but many times it's not. To expect exhilaration is to make ourselves "pleasure-addicts." This in itself will block the development of a deeply enthusiastic attitude. Real enthusiasm can only develop and grow to maturity in a personality that seeks to be free—free of compulsive behavior, irrational thinking, incorrect imagery, unnecessary negative emotion, and the need for immediate gratification.

A number of years ago, I was having lunch in Philadelphia with an editor. He told me he could tell the difference between someone who had successfully endured a lot in life and someone who hadn't. When

I asked him how he could discern this difference, he said that the former type of person was deeper in his or her emotions and wasn't superficial in the joy and sadness being experienced. Spiritual guides help us avoid a surface exhilaration or a pseudo-positive thinking mode. They remind us that a grateful, open, assertive, and free approach to the world opens up opportunities for the deep personal joy and peace that is even possible amidst the reality of suffering.

As the author John Gardner aptly pointed out a number of years ago: "We are all continually faced with a series of great opportunities, brilliantly disguised as insoluble problems." The point being made here is that when our eyes are opened and the "Aha!" experience dawns, we are able to put things in perspective and embrace enthusiasm. Thus, annoyances remain annoyances and don't move into the realm of preoccupations that pull us down; therefore, we are able to appreciate the gift of perspective in our lives.

Perspective and enthusiasm go hand-in-hand. You can't have one without the other. Perspective loosens up our perceptions so as to allow the important issues to take precedence in a world frequently caught up in false agendas. These false agendas blur the line between what is essential (i.e., relationships, peace, love) and what isn't (i.e., inordinate power, concern with one's image, competition, accomplishments).

The following letter written by a first-year college student to her father during the middle of her second semester, delightfully points this out. Prior to receiving this note, her father was totally preoccupied with her "success" in college. He was worried because she didn't do well in her first semester and was concerned she would fail out during the second semester—and take his money with her! He had forgotten, as many of us parents do, that performance in courses is only a partial measure of learning; moreover, there is much more to the total college experience that just grades.

Despite her youth, this young woman knew this better than he, and so taught him an important lesson on perspective. On the front page of her note it said:

Dear Dad,

Everything is going well here at college this semester, so you can stop worrying. I am very, very happy now . . . you would love Ichabod. He is a wonderful, wonderful man and our first three months of marriage have been blissful.

And more good news Dad. The drug rehab program we are both in just told us that the twins that are due soon will not be addicted at birth.

Having read this, her father then turned the page with trepidation. On the other side of the note it said:

Now, Dad, there actually is no Ichabod. I'm not married nor pregnant. And I haven't ever abused

drugs. But I did get a D in chemistry, so keep
things in perspective![68]

Spiritual guides help us open up to life so we can
be in a better position to more clearly reflect on the
perils to, and the seeds of, perspective and enthusiasm. Spiritual guides can then help us to recapture
the simplicity that is born of seeing life not merely
as something to "succeed at" but as something to
experience fully and freely as God would wish it. This
undertaking must be a daily prayerful effort, supported by others who are graced and gifted, if we are not
to lose our way—a real possibility given the demands
and unhealthy lures of modern life.

TYPES OF GUIDES

We have seen how spiritual guides help us uncover
and deal with our fears, appreciate what we need to
be detached from, and instill in us a sense of renewed
perspective and enthusiasm. But what types of "spiritual friends" might be helpful in this regard? I would
like to cluster my response to the question under four
headings: *mentor/director; spiritual companion; spiritual
amma* or *abba*; and *books* and *places*.

SPIRITUAL DIRECTORS OR MENTORS

The first of this group is the person usually titled a
"spiritual director" or "mentor." This person is probably the most familiar of the group, especially in

Catholic, Orthodox, Anglican, Methodist, and Lutheran confessions of faith. The focus of the encounter with this type of guide is our relationship with God and all this entails. Meetings occur on a regular basis and are primarily concerned with strengthening our covenant with God in a way that results in our being more integrated as persons and more open to interacting with and serving others.

In many cases, persons filling the role of spiritual mentor or director have received both "a call" from God and formal preparation through studies in spirituality, forms of prayer, sacred scriptures, theology, and applied psychology. However, this need not always be the case. The charism of being a director is freely given by God to whomever the creator pleases. As a result, we sometimes see people in this role who have actually not gone through formal or specific education to prepare for this work. Yet, they have been given the gift and the Lord draws to them people who are in search of a more intimate relationship with God.

Conversely, there are some well-credentialed directors who clearly do not have the call; their emotional energy is primarily directed at trying to shore up their own psychological defenses and meet their own needs. Thus little is available to be put at the service of those who are seeking their guidance. Consequently, the choice of someone to fill this role in our life is sometimes quite difficult.

Given this, a suggestion in seeking out a spiritual director is to ask for recommendations from people whose judgment we respect in this area (i.e., friends knowledgeable about spiritual direction, members of the pastoral team serving the parish, diocesan offices of adult spirituality or family life). In many cases, the spiritually mature persons in our lives can lead us to those who can be helpful in our desire to be intentional about the development of our prayer life. However, the process of selecting a director may still take several tries, so in the search one needs to remember to be prayerful, prudent, patient, and persistent.

SPIRITUAL COMPANIONS

A "spiritual companion" is another type of guide who, amidst the confusion, complexity, stress, boredom, and pain of modern existence, can foster an increase in the development of meaning in our lives. In this category are those people who call us to be all that we can be without embarrassing us because we presently are where we are. Even though we may only see these persons once in a while or speak only rarely of specifically "religious" matters with them, there is a sense of feeling nourished, awake, and reconnected to life when we leave them.

We may have certain persons who fill this informal role the whole of our lives. In other cases, there are individuals who fill this role early in life but whom we outgrow in later adulthood. We can often determine this based on how nourished and challenged we feel after speaking with them. With respect to this, the following words from a fifth century desert father may be helpful: "In the beginning when we got together we used to talk about something that was good for our souls, and we went up and up, and ascended even to heaven. But now we get together and spend our time in criticizing everything, and we drag one another down into the abyss." Given this, it may be helpful to ask ourselves who in our present circle of friends continues to provide companionship in the search to be connected with the will of God.

SPIRITUAL AMMAS AND ABBAS

"Spiritual ammas and abbas" (mothers and fathers) compromise the next grouping of guides that we may need at certain times in our lives. The essential point to remember about this type of spiritual friend is that persons such as these are usually only called upon at certain turning points in our lives. We may consult such wise and holy people once or only a few times during our life to help us discern a major turn in direction, as a check on the way we have understood our calling, or to review the focus of our life's work.

For instance, Henri Nouwen related that at one point on a visit to Mother Teresa, he asked her what she felt he must do to be a good priest. Years after this, when he was at Harvard, I in turn asked him how I should relate to God in order to nourish my relationship with God and my role as a pastoral psychologist who worked primarily with people in ministry. Both his question of Mother Teresa and my question of him were asked at important points in our lives and the answers we received were different given the great variance in our situations.

The important factors to remember with respect to seeking out a wise and holy person to ask for help at crucial junctures in life are: 1) We only seek such special assistance when there is a real need and we have already utilized and found somewhat wanting all existing supports in our lives, including our own personal resources (i.e., problem-solving, reflection, prayer). 2) We need to be serious in our request for information and not just inquisitive (some people are continually asking for "a word" from these spiritual figures without weighing the gravity of their request). 3) Take special care in selecting someone who we feel will be of real benefit to us now. There is an old Russian proverb that states: "The hammer shatters glass but forges steel." A sage who can be of real help to one person at certain junctures in life may be of no assistance to him or her at another point or be of no help at all to other types of individuals who seek help. Only Jesus could respond to all who came to him. 4) Recognize that we might not like, or immediately understand, what we are told. Once again, even Jesus had many persons who came to him who did not react positively to his answers to their questions.

BOOKS AND PLACES

A final category of "friends" that have often proven to be helpful to many of us are actually not living persons with whom we relate. Instead, they are the messages and support from God which are offered to us in some of the particular books we read and which are reflected in certain places we visit.

With respect to our readings, surprisingly this type of "friendship" may be more important than one might expect. In some cases, given our situation in life at the time, the word of God may even come to us primarily through our readings. And so, in some instances to avoid such opportunities as these for grace can even dangerously stunt the maturity of our spiritual life.

I have found that more often than not when people who are in ministry come to me for a visit to discuss some stress or anxiety they are experiencing in life, they have all but given up reading books that would help them break through the type of thinking in which they are trapped. In reality, sacred scripture and other readings, including the spiritual classics, are actually essential for most of us if we are to maintain a continued sense of perspective and freshness in our attitude toward life.

When feeling lost and spiritually cold, a few good words from a spiritually rich volume can fan the embers of hope and clarity in us. Avoiding them doesn't make sense, even if, maybe especially if, we seem to feel "down" or too upset to sit and read. In such instances, I suggest to myself and others not to listen to one's negative thoughts but instead to: 1) sit down in spite of one's hesitant or discouraged feelings; 2) quiet oneself by closing one's eyes; 3) recite a short prayer; 4) open up one's eyes then and read a few lines from a book one has found to be a good companion in the past (maybe the lines one underlined in a recent reading); 5) ponder these words slowly and with gentle respect. The results are usually positive.

Although we don't hear much about it today, the places we visit and those in which we live and work are also important with respect to the development of our spiritual life. It need not be a special place of pilgrimage that is famous; it could be merely a rock by the ocean or a street in our home town. But there are places in our lives that reminds us of the Lord and in which we seem to breathe more easily and understand God's wishes for us more clearly. Therefore, not to heighten our awareness of such places and to avoid visiting them personally or through imagery, seems foolish. For example, a particular hospital chapel in New York City and a certain small lake surrounded by mountains in Newfoundland were, and still are, special places of peace for me. When feeling uncentered in prayer, I often recall them in my mind's eye and they help me settle down.

I also find that visiting places where others have experienced significant encounters with God is good for me as well. That is why when I come to lead a retreat or workshop for a community of persons in ministry, I will usually spend some time in their chapel, a place that has been the setting over the years of great prayers and tears of joy, sadness, anguish, and hope. These places have a special history of encounter with God in which we can participate in some significant way if only we have the desire and take the time.

Many of the places we have been and will go in the future, can be wonderful settings in which to meet God if only we are open to the Lord's surprising presence in them. Not to be sensitive in this way and to only wait instead for future "special" opportunities in which to experience God (e.g., a retreat/day of recollection) would seem to be a waste of some of the gifts God graces us with every day, if only we have the intention and expend the little bit of energy necessary to avail ourselves of them.

We can only appreciate ourselves as God intended us to be when we begin to better value the gift of ordinariness. The beauty of ordinariness is especially revealed, supported, and enhanced by the presence of good friends. The prophet, cheerleader, harasser, and an array of spiritual guides make up an interpersonal web that embraces, challenges, and directs us in our journey towards God, especially during the most difficult of times for ourselves and those whom we love.

The following Vietnamese folk tale sums up the import and tone of what has been described in this chapter:

> In hell, people have chopsticks a yard long so they cannot reach their mouths; and so, are forever suffering a hunger that will never be quieted. Whereas, in heaven even though the chopsticks are the same length, everyone is still always well-fed. The reason for this is simple: In heaven, the people feed one another.[69]

This is, indeed, the real lesson each of us must appreciate about the value of true friendship, and the one to recall every day as we continue on our search to discover God anew within ourselves and in the people around us.

Five

A SIMPLE CARING PRESENCE

There is little doubt that friendship is a beautiful gift to share and experience. And, certainly it is true that "a friend is someone who knows the song in your heart, and can sing it back to you when you've forgotten how it goes."[70] Yet, being a true friend to someone can also be quite difficult. People normally have so many personal agendas, needs, and expectations that the friendship given or received is usually conditional. Consequently, the sensitivity needed for true friendship is frequently distorted by a sea of conditions, prejudices, demands, and personal insecurities.

Maybe this is why sound self-esteem fosters good friendship and true ordinariness is experienced as tangible holiness. When we are in a relationship that is real, open, and unconditional, we can sense the presence of God. So, rather than game-playing or anxious positioning in our interactions, a free and life-giving atmosphere can develop. When the ordinariness-in-me encounters the ordinariness-in-you, the results can be quite life-giving and "extra-ordinary."

Relationships based on ordinariness grow when fed by attitudes such as openness, humility, simplicity, prayerfulness, vulnerability, perseverance, and sensitivity. With these attributes we will have the necessary strength to be fully present to others, to truly listen to "the song in their hearts."

OPENNESS

There is an old saying from India: "When you have once been bitten by a snake, you become even cautious of a rope."[71] Hurt is so much a part of being in a relationship that it is difficult for many of us to open ourselves to others. We may even question whether it is worth all the trouble and effort. Friendship is a risk many of us don't wish to take.

Even with sound self-esteem (based on a sense that God loves us for who we are as ordinary people), we may still make the mistake of holding back emotionally from others and deny ourselves the true value of community. As Alexander Solzhenitsyn, the Russian author, once said: "We do not err because the truth is difficult to see. It is visible at a glance. We err because it is more comfortable [to avoid it]."

The following Jewish tale illustrates that perseverance in our efforts to be open to all people is a requirement of living "in the Light." There can be no half-steps in our willingness to be open to friendship.

An old Rabbi once asked his pupils how they could tell when the night had ended and the day had begun.

"Could it be," asked one of the students, "when you can see an animal in the distance and tell whether it's sheep or a dog?"

"No," answered the Rabbi.

Another asked, "Is it when you can look at a tree in the distance and tell whether it's a fig tree or a peach tree?"

"No," answered the Rabbi.

"Then when is it?" the pupils demanded.

"It is when you can look on the face of any man or woman and see that it is your sister or brother. Because if you cannot see this, it is still night."[72]

But even though we may accept that openness is important, a practical question still remains for us: What would help us to remain open to others and be less defensive in situations that we perceive as personally difficult or threatening?

One way of responding to this question is by providing a check on ourselves with respect to our openness and defensiveness. And a good way to do this is to reflect at the end of the day on our specific interactions with others. We can either do this mentally (on our walk or drive home) or by keeping a journal. The following is a checklist of some of the types of questions that can be reviewed as part of such a daily stock-taking.

A Checklist on Openness

- When and with whom did I not feel spontaneous in my reactions today and what were the topics being discussed? In these instances how do I understand my behavior, feelings, thoughts, and images? Focus on learning about yourself— not on blaming or excusing your behavior. Blaming yourself will only short-circuit self-understanding because behavior that you wince at will eventually turn into behavior that you will wink at. On the other hand, assigning blame to others only leads to projecting a number of one's own issues onto someone else; this in the end has obvious serious drawbacks because in giving away the blame, we in turn give away the power to have an impact on the situation as well. After all, if a problem is due completely to someone else's attitude or actions, there is little left we can do to improve it.

- Was I defensive today? Did I feel angry, hurt, annoyed, anxious, sad, disappointed, rigid, passive, overly nice, judgmental, bored, distracted, confused, impatient, or un-empathic today? If so, what can I understand about such defensiveness that will also teach me something about myself?

- Did I deal with a situation today by avoiding communication in one of the following ways?

  1. Attacking the person directly or indirectly (e.g., passive-aggressiveness which involves obstructionist tendencies, procrastination and other subtle ways of impedance);

  2. Exaggerating what was going on;

  3. Hiding behind the rules or some technicality as a way of avoiding communication;

  4. Diverting the attention by bringing in some unrelated issue;

5. Retreating into "chronic niceness" or within a shell of silence.

Each of us can develop our own informal set of questions to check on personal defensiveness. By reviewing questions such as these we can gain a greater understanding of ourselves and thus be in a better position both psychologically and spiritually to increase our openness. Specifically, we will be able to:

- Uncover many of our "emotional weak spots" (those subjects about which we are most sensitive);

- Ferret out some of our hidden anxieties (fear of anger, not being liked, being dismissed as a valuable person, not being seen as unique, being viewed as weak, etc.);

- Bring to the fore the inappropriate expectations we may have of others (e.g., if people like me they must agree with all my opinions);

- Uncover some of the major prejudices or "isms" we have that are hidden from us (e.g., sexism, ageism, racism, clericalism);

- Highlight the emotional "baggage" or unfinished business we are still carrying around with us.

Such a review is not done for the purpose of self-condemnation. It is done before a loving God with the desire to find out more about ourselves so we can: 1) have more concrete personal knowledge in order to free the energy being used for defensiveness and make it available for creativity and growth; 2) be a stronger, more sensitive friend to others; 3) be more open to receiving the truth, and thus meeting God in self, others, and during our moments of silence and solitude with the Lord.

HUMILITY AND SIMPLICITY

In addition to openness, our ability to offer friendship is fostered as well when we embrace the gift of ordinariness through an appreciation of humility. Too often we fail in relationships because we are not willing to accept the wonderful yet limited gifts we have to offer others. Instead, we often feel we are "not enough" as persons. We believe we must be able to do the spectacular or otherwise risk rejection.

And so, frequently we get frustrated when our effort to be amazing by trying to meet everyone's needs, no matter how great they are, fails. Our Herculean efforts can take an incredible toll on our energy and resources. When we fall into this kind of "savior complex" behavior, we have failed to remember an important lesson. "Do not forget," wrote Teilhard de Chardin, "that the value and interest of life is not so much to do conspicuous things . . . as to do ordinary things with the perception of their enormous value."

Often all that is called for in friendship is a listening ear and a simple reaction, but we are tempted to blow things out of proportion. If we can take a cue from those people in our life and society who are able to model simplicity it would be very helpful for us. The famous New York Yankee catcher Yogi Berra, for example, was once confronted by a young outfielder with a puzzling, seemingly insurmountable problem about his hitting. The youth said: "I'm in a rut! I can't seem to break the habit of swinging up at the ball!" Yogi looked at him, scratched his head, blinked, and said: "Well, try swinging down."

Although dramatic actions are sometimes necessary, they are not the essence of friendship. Not are they the sign of our being worthwhile, caring members of the community we call "the people of God." A simple sharing of self is. The following comparison goes to the heart of the matter by visually making this point clear:

> In a cemetery somewhere in the United States, there are two gravestones placed right next to each other. One is a large imposing marker for a deceased general. It lists all of the battles he was in as well as many, many of his other accomplishments.

> Next to this large stone is a small one erected for a young woman who died when she was only

21 years old. And the inscription her husband had engraved on it is only one line. It says simply:

"Everywhere she went she brought flowers."[73]

This is what I think all of us are called to do in our own way: to discover and offer "flowers"—our unique, God-given talents—to others. But to do this we must be willing to accept our own and others' human limitations and frailties. Otherwise, we will forget to discover our real gifts and choose only to do what we believe will serve to impress and satisfy, rather than encourage and nourish.

LIMITATIONS

In giving simply of ourselves we must discern our own and others' human capabilities without disdain and face the great difficulty of being willing to both give and let go. Anthony de Mello expresses part of this theme in the following outrageous story which uses exaggeration as a way of helping us accept our own limits and curbing the unrealistic expectations we have of others.

> The disciples could not understand the seemingly arbitrary manner in which some people were accepted for discipleship and others were rejected. They got a clue one day when they heard the master say, "Don't attempt to teach a pig to sing. It wastes your time, and irritates [the heck out of] the pig."[74]

In the process of accepting others' limits and letting go, we must be sensitive to our own sometimes narrow, insensitive belief that only we have the answer to others' questions and life problems. Dorothy Day points this out with respect to the young. She says: "Young, bright, idealistic, people are tempted in a special way by arrogance. The ambition they have to change the world can turn into a bullying of others and a terrible habit of patronizing everyone but themselves."[75]

I think this danger is present not only with the young, but with all of us who care and want to make the world a better place in which to live. Consequently, humility and patience are watchwords for those who would be caring persons. As we know and have probably experienced ourselves, much harm can inadvertently be done in the name of good!

A Prayerful Presence

Another reality of friendship for us to embrace today is the beauty and value of being a simple caring presence to people. In many cases, we (and those with whom we interact) feel that somehow the relationship is not strong enough if there are not frequent interpersonal exchanges. However, if it is valid that true ordinariness is tangible holiness, then one's ordinary presence is usually enough. But as we will see in the following story, the problem is in both recognizing and accepting this reality.

> A gruff, loveable priest in Alaska learned this lesson when he was assigned to be chaplain in a residential school for Eskimo children. One evening he was sitting in his room working at the desk when one of the youths appeared at the door asking to come into his room.

> He responded: "No. I'm busy." The youth persisted: "Father, I won't bother you." The priest finally relented and said: "OK, come in, but don't bother me!" The youth came in sat down on the floor, leaned against the bed and stayed there quietly for about an hour. At which point he got up and said: "I am going to bed now Father, good night."

> He did this repeatedly for almost eight months. The priest occasionally would offer him a magazine to read, but the youth would always decline.

> Finally, the priest recognized what was happening: the Eskimo boy just wanted to be there with him. That was enough. It was the priest's simple presence that was needed and enjoyed.[76]

In order to offer a simple caring presence and to be a friend to others in need we must also seek to have a prayerful sense of self. For when this is the case in our lives, the love we have for God and self can blossom.

Then the inconsequential in our lives loses power and we can be psychologically and spiritually free to welcome all types of people, no matter what their mood, background, occupation, or status.

But the topic of "prayerfulness" or "prayer"—as can be seen in the following enjoyable apocryphal story—is an elusive one, not as easy to address as one would hope.

> A very famous rabbi was on his death bed and there was a line of students at his bedside. Right next to his bed was his greatest student, then the next most accomplished, all the way down the line to the end where the last student who was barely getting through rabbinical school stood.
>
> The most intelligent student asked the rabbi: "Before you die is there a lesson you can share with us?"
>
> To this the rabbi nodded affirmatively and said: "Remember that prayer is like a river."
>
> The brightest student was struck with awe, nodded gravely, and then passed this on to the next student in line who in turn passed it on until it was told to the last student who listened, scratched his head and responded: "What does the rabbi mean that prayer is like a river?"
>
> The student who told him turned to the next person in line and relayed the question until it got

to the brightest one who, when he also couldn't
answer the question, in turn asked the rabbi:
"Rabbi, what do you mean that prayer is like a
river?"

To which the rabbi shrugged and responded:
"OK, so prayer is not like a river."[77]

Although much can be said about prayer, it is, in
the end, not what we say or know that matters. What
matters is what we do. I want to make a brief nota-
tion once again about the particular relevance of quiet
morning prayer for those of us who would seek to be a
caring presence to others. To be involved with God the
first thing each day centers us on what is important. In
addition, it helps us to be awake to the day stretching
out before us, one which may be our last. And finally,
morning silence and solitude can enable us to better
come to our senses and be in the now. This is especially important so we don't miss those interpersonal
encounters that might bring us closer to God if we
weren't nostalgically reflecting on the past or preoccupied with the future.

But above all, it is the quiet prayerful space of the
early morning that enables us to be better attuned to
God's particular call for us each day. Without such an
intentional space for prayer, hearing the "voice" of
God becomes quite difficult. For, as we are constantly
reminded by spiritual writers: "There's always music

amongst the trees in the garden, but our hearts must be very quiet to hear it."[78]

VULNERABILITY

Vulnerability is also important if we wish to be open to relationships because we will experience real risks with intimacy. To help us be able to appreciate this I offer the following starkly honest statement by a psychologist speaking about the implications of therapeutic involvement with one's patients. He notes:

> Most therapists understand that they jeopardize their own emotional well being when they intimately encounter the pain of others. Never mind that we catch [our patients'] colds and flus, what about their pessimism, [their] negativity? You cannot see somebody week after week, listen to their stories, and dry their tears without being profoundly affected by the experience. There are risks for the therapist he will not recognize until years later. Images stay with us to the grave. Words creep back to haunt us. Those silent screams remain deafening.[79]

Interactions for most people will usually not be as broad or intense as the ones psychotherapists or counselors experience with their patients. Still, by thinking about our own relationships with family, friends, and others to whom we have reached out in the past, I'm sure we can all easily recall illustrations and memories of difficult, hurtful experiences we have had. Relationships can certainly bring joy, but they also require a willingness to experience the pain of intimacy and growth.

Real relationship does not come without risk or vulnerability. And, as the following Sufi tale poetically points out (in a slightly different way from the psychologist just quoted), while this can be quite frightening, it is sometimes exactly what is required if we wish to live the spiritual life more fully, with a sense of surrender and trust.

> A stream was working itself across the country, experiencing little difficulty. It ran around the rocks and through the mountains. Then it arrived at a desert. Just as it had crossed every other barrier, the stream tried to cross this one, but it found that as fast as it rain into the sand, its waters disappeared. After many attempts it became very discouraged. It appeared that there was no way it could continue the journey.

> Then a voice came in the wind. "If you stay the way you are you cannot cross the sands, you cannot become more than a quagmire. To go further you will have to lose yourself."

> "But if I lose myself," the stream cried, "I will never know what I'm supposed to be."

"Oh, on the contrary," said the voice, "if you lose yourself you will become more than you ever dreamed you could be."

So the stream surrendered to the drying sun. And the clouds into which it was formed were carried by the raging wind for miles. Once it crossed the desert, the stream poured down from the skies, fresh and clean, and full of the energy that comes from storms.[80]

Even though vulnerability is frightening at times, it can lead to new possibilities for us. Specifically, the process of meeting others with a deep sense of openness will place us in a unique position to achieve greater self-awareness by encountering new, previously hidden parts of ourselves. As the historian Jean Leclerc said of St. Francis:

In opening himself to the world, in taking his place among the creatures, in becoming profoundly aware of them as "brother" and "sister," Francis also opened himself to that obscure part of himself which is rooted in nature; unconsciously he was fraternizing with his own depth.

So as we listen to others in a world which seems to no longer want to listen, we begin not only to hear the voices of others but also to become more sensitive to our own inner voices as well. We recognize the paradox that we can't truly know our own story in any rich detail until we are willing to listen closely as others tell theirs.

Sensitive Listening

Anthony Hopkins' tribute to Sir Laurence Olivier in the *New York Times* a few years ago included a number of statements, but it seemed to focus in particular on the great actor's sensitivity and "listening presence" to others. Hopkins described his first meeting with Olivier:

> He came forward to shake my hand and I gave him my name. He gave me his full attention. This was an ability of his, to give his full, undivided attention to the moment, as if there were no past or future. Even in his "ordinariness" there was that one peculiar quality of concentration. This is what set him apart as an extraordinary human being: he never dismissed anything, he never disregarded anything. Everything held his attention.[81]

When we are truly sensitive to others we offer them the gift of a listening presence similar to Olivier's. And this gift is so precious because it offers a number of potential interpersonal rewards that are so desperately needed today. Among them are:

- A chance to really be heard. Today everyone seems to have "answers," but few seem available to listen.

- An opportunity for people to let their feelings out ("catharsis") in front of someone who is not afraid of their expression of emotion. This shows the hurting person that there is no need to be overly anxious about being aware of his or her own feelings.

- A possibility for the development of a trusting relationship. This is so because in the process of sharing intimate ideas with someone who accepts them unconditionally, an emotional "bridge" is built between the participants.

- A time to enable the start of problem-solving behavior. By expressing their feelings and thoughts clearly and in reviewing their behavior, a wealth of information can come to the fore to be examined and understood as a preliminary step to taking meaningful action.

But being an effective listener is not easy. Many of us judge people automatically so much of the time that without even knowing it we have stopped listening and started evaluating before those who have come to us have had a real chance to express themselves fully. In addition, for most of us the discipline necessary to listen is often not very well-developed so we only get partial bits of information or confuse facts with impressions or interpretations. Furthermore, at times, we also just don't want to expend the energy necessary to ask questions if we are confused. We often say to ourselves: "It won't help." "She or he may get angry if I ask this." "I don't want to appear foolish or seem that I wasn't listening carefully enough in the first place."

The art of listening takes energy, courage, and much practice. When one famous television interviewer was asked how he had developed his interviewing skill, he responded by saying that one's questions are only as good as one's ability to first listen carefully to what is said. He said he took great pains to be sensitive to the information he heard and not to let pass what others might disregard, ignore, or not attend to because they were not really listening.

And so, given the above interviewer's comment, I wish to offer a "mini-review" of a few of the more accepted simple disciplines needed to be more sensitive listeners.

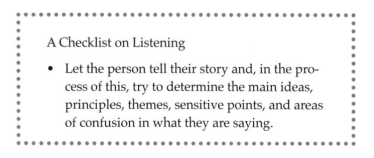

A Checklist on Listening

- Let the person tell their story and, in the process of this, try to determine the main ideas, principles, themes, sensitive points, and areas of confusion in what they are saying.

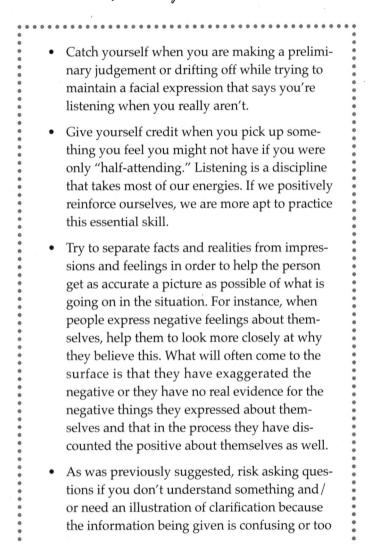

- Catch yourself when you are making a preliminary judgement or drifting off while trying to maintain a facial expression that says you're listening when you really aren't.

- Give yourself credit when you pick up something you feel you might not have if you were only "half-attending." Listening is a discipline that takes most of our energies. If we positively reinforce ourselves, we are more apt to practice this essential skill.

- Try to separate facts and realities from impressions and feelings in order to help the person get as accurate a picture as possible of what is going on in the situation. For instance, when people express negative feelings about themselves, help them to look more closely at why they believe this. What will often come to the surface is that they have exaggerated the negative or they have no real evidence for the negative things they expressed about themselves and that in the process they have discounted the positive about themselves as well.

- As was previously suggested, risk asking questions if you don't understand something and/or need an illustration of clarification because the information being given is confusing or too general. If the person reacts negatively—"You mean after all I told you, you still don't understand?"—let the negative feelings pass you by. Respond that you really would like to understand better and ask their patience.

To be sensitive to other persons by giving them an opportunity to share their joy and sadness, their history and the issues they may be facing today can be a lot of work! However when we really take the *energy* to listen to another's story not only do they gain, but we do as well.

Matina S. Horner, president of Radcliffe College, wrote:

> Fine [written] biographies give us both a glimpse of ourselves and a reflection of the human spirit. [They] create lifelong models for us. Reading about other people's experiences encourages us to persist, to face hardship, and to feel less alone. Biography tell us about choice, the power of a personal vision, and the interdependence of human life.[82]

The same can be said about those of us who persevere in our interactions with others in an effort to listen to, and understand, the "oral biographies" of people who come to us to discuss their journey.

And so, when we make the effort to be a sensitive listener, the rewards are there for both parties (although sometimes they may not be evident on first blush). So, the effort to "stay the journey" on our part is crucial and we must constantly ask ourselves when we are tempted to give up: "Did I fail . . . or did I fail to try long and hard enough to this point?"

PERSEVERANCE

In the Koran the message is simple: "God helps those who persevere." Contemporary philosophers, psychologists, spiritual figures, and existentialist writers have certainly supported this ancient theme. As the poet Henry Wadsworth Longfellow once noted with his usual dry humor: "Perseverance is a great element of success. If you only knock long enough at the gate, you are sure to wake up somebody!"

At the heart of perseverance is our constant prayer asking God to strengthen this important gift in us. However, in addition to asking for this grace, we must obviously do our part in trying to remain committed—a point which is humorously illustrated in the following story that Anthony de Mello loved to tell on his lecture tours around the world.

> Toward the end of his life a rabbi was exhausted and prayed to God that his last days might be

made easier and financially secure. So, he asked God that he might win the lottery. So, he prayed and prayed and prayed constantly about this.

Weeks passed. Months passed. Then years passed. And finally he screamed out in frustration and desperation: "God, give me a break!"

To which God answered: "Give me a break yourself. Buy a ticket!"

Perseverance then is something we must both pray for and take action upon in our own behalf if we are to be able to continue in our efforts to build up community through friendship with others.

Too often I have seen people crushed under the weight of relationships. There are times I have had a similar feeling myself. I have gotten up in the morning tired and discouraged, and looked in the mirror and said to myself: "That's it. I've met enough people in my life. I must have met hundreds, no thousands. I've met enough! Off to the hermitage I go with twelve quarts of Ben and Jerry's *Cherry Garcia* ice cream."

To some degree the problem for me and others is not only that we have forgotten to pray, but also that we have failed to take the basic steps for psychophysiological survival. Like the rabbi in the story, we must go "buy a ticket." We must see what *we* can do to prepare for difficult or intense encounters with others in order to prevent personal emotional and spiritual burnout.

While there are entire books available on the topic of stress, I wish to offer at least an outline of what I consider the main necessary skills. They are essential for personal care of our own psychological and physical well-being and I feel we need to know, remember, and practice them if we wish to remain actively compassionate people. While we may be informed about stress and agree we should do something about it, we may still feel overwhelmed. The sheer volume of material available on stress might overwhelm us, with the result that we continue living in the same old way.

However, knowing this natural tendency, I think if we are willing to read and reflect occasionally on the following several simple points culled from the stress literature, gradual progress is more realistically possible. As the famous writer of western novels Louis L'Amour said before his death: "Victory is not won in miles but in inches. Win a little now, hold your ground, and later win a little more."

STRESS MANAGEMENT

PHYSICAL HEALTH

1. *Sleep:* Without enough sleep the quality of what you do will decrease; rising early requires going to bed at a reasonable hour.

2. *Food:* Eating three light meals, at a reasonable pace, and being mindful of the nutritional value in what you eat is one of the best ways to keep weight down and nourishment and energy up.

3. *Exercise:* Taking a fairly brisk walk each day is a good minimum exercise. Doing it on a consistent basis is better than some irregular or future extensive exercise plan which we fail at and feel guilty about.

4. *Leisure:* Relaxing with your feet up and/or being involved in activities that provide genuine enjoyment are not niceties of physical health. Rather, they are undervalued but essential building blocks to good health. Leisure helps us "flow" with life's joys, and problems in a more accepting philosophical way.

5. *Pacing:* Taking a little more time to get places makes the trip more relaxing; stopping every hour or hour and a half to get out of the car and stretch on long trips makes them a lot more enjoyable and helps increase stamina. Likewise, taking breaks when you feel the need makes your productivity better. The important lesson here is to use any technique necessary to slow yourself down so you don't rush to the grave missing the scenery in your life along the way.

PSYCHOLOGICAL STABILITY

1. *Laughter:* If laughter is good medicine, then surely laughing at yourself is healing. We all tend to take ourselves too seriously. So, doing something about this can significantly reduce unnecessary stress and help improve one's perspective on self and life.

2. *Values:* Know what is important and what isn't; by knowing what you believe to be really important you can choose easily and well between alternatives.

3. *Control:* Be careful to discern between what you can control and what you can't; while worrying about something when it happens is natural, continuing to preoccupy yourself with it is not. When you catch yourself worrying endlessly, tease yourself that you must be "the world's best worrier." Then plan what you can do about it, and let it go. If and when it comes up again; review the process until it lessens or stops. This technique may need a good deal of practice for it to "take root" in your attitude.

4. *Self-Appreciation:* Reflect on what gifts God has given you, recall them each day in detail (make a list if you have to on paper), and be grateful for them by promising to nurture and share

them—not in a compulsive manner but in a generous way. By this I mean have low expectations that people will respond as you would wish or appreciate your efforts. However, simultaneously still try to maintain high hopes that you can appreciate how God is working through both of you in every relationship. Also, use multiple measures of "success" in your work so you don't miss the good that is occurring before you because of a narrow, success-oriented viewpoint. For instance, too often we measure what we achieve at the end of a process and fail to see or value appropriately all of the good we did along the way.

5. *Involvement . . . not Overinvolvement:* Be active in what you feel is meaningful (the kind of things you would be pleased to reflect on at the very end of life—not necessarily those things that others might feel are impressive or important). Assertiveness on your part, both to volunteer to be involved in what you believe is good and to say no to demands that aren't, is also an essential part of increasing your involvement in stimulating activities and curbing (wherever possible) ones that are personally draining.

6. *Support Group:* Have people in your life who care; contact them frequently by phone and in

writing as well as in person. Ideally, among this group should be a variety of psychologically healthy friends who can challenge, support, encourage, teach, and make you laugh.

7. *Escape:* There are times when we should "run away" because facing things directly in all of our relationships all the time would be debilitating. To do this you can use novels, breaks during the day, movies, walks, hobbies (fishing, bicycle riding, etc.).

8. *Be Spontaneous:* A small creative action or change during the day or week can make life much more fun. This is a lot more practical than waiting for a yearly vacation.

9. *Be Careful of Negativity:* Often we hear negative comments like thunder and praise like a whisper. Use self-talk to catch your own negative tendencies (i.e., to see things in black-and-white terms, to exaggerate the negative, to let one negative event contaminate the whole day or week, or to discount other positive events). Then answer these thoughts with more accurate positive ones. For example, if you feel slightly depressed and check your thinking, you may see that because one thing went wrong today, you are saying to yourself that you are really a failure at what you do. By recognizing this

exaggeration as nonsense, you can tell yourself more correctly that you made a mistake, not that you are a mistake! Following this, you can then recall successes you have had and bring to mind the faces of those who have been grateful for your presence in their lives. This will show you the face of a loving God in the world and help break the back of the strong seamless negative thinking you are under at the time. Remember, negative thinking takes a good deal of energy. Stop it, and a great deal of energy will be freed up for growth and enjoyment.

10. *Check Your Individual Balance in the Areas of:*

a. stimulation and quiet,

b. reflection and action,

c. work and leisure,

d. self-care and care of others,

e. self-improvement and patience,

f. future aspirations and present positive realities,

g. involvement and detachment.

ORDINARINESS AND FRIENDSHIP

Neither availability to others in general, nor being an *anamchara* (soul friend) with certain people in particular, is easy. Yet, if we really do wish to live deeply spiritual lives ourselves, and to help others live this way in today's confusing times, there is no alternative to expending the necessary energy required in being a sensitive friend to others in need.

As Peig Sayers, who lives in the Blasket Islands off the coast of Ireland (where there are very few trees and little protection from the harsh Atlantic wind), wisely recognizes: "It is in the shelter of each other that people live."[83]

Therefore, as ordinary persons banded together in a world which is now so small, we must learn to face each other in understanding and love. However, to do this we also must be realistic and have the humility to pray each day for patience, wisdom, charity, and forgiveness—not only of others' failings but of our own as well. Otherwise we will quickly become disillusioned by our own shortcomings and the limitations of others when our day-to-day interactions don't reflect the hopes we had for them.

True intimacy can cause confusion as often as clarity; it produces disagreement along with harmony; it results in exhaustion sometimes well equal to the exhilaration we may experience. The simple truth, which all of us know, is that sharing and receiving love in concrete ways is often painful. Real relationships are obviously not as pretty as old romantic movies would sometimes have us believe.

As a matter of fact, that is why true friendship is something some of us either only wish for or shy away from most of the time—even when that friendship is with our God! Rabbi Heschel appreciates this:

> [A person's] plight is not due to the fear of non-being [or] to the fear of death, but to the fear of living, because all living is branded with unerasable shock at [the] absurdity, cruelty, and callousness experienced in the past. A human being is a being in fear of pain, in fear of being put to shame. The fear of living arises most commonly out of experiences of failure or insult, of having gone astray or having been rebuffed. It is rooted in the encounter with other human beings, in not knowing how to be with other beings, in the inability or refuse to communicate, but above all in the failure to live in complete involvement with what transcends our living.[84]

However, despite the true pain of intimacy, it is in honest friendship that we really learn about ourselves. It is in real relationship that (although our own-fashioned images are sometimes bruised) our God-given ordinariness is continually rediscovered in some profound way.

So, it is understandable if sometimes dreaming about friendship and a deep relationship with God may seem more pleasant than actually trying to seek it. And, it is easy to see that reading about the spiritual life may appear more gratifying and safer than attempting to live it.

But, despite such natural temptations, I think most of us know in our hearts that it is in the actual occurrence of the ordinariness-in-me meeting the ordinariness-in-you that real encounter with God is frequently made possible in daily life. And we are clearly reminded of this in the following beautiful, direct, and challenging passage from the first letter of John:

> If God loved us so much, we too should love each other. No one has ever seen God, but as long as we love each other God remains in us and his love comes to its perfection in us. This is the proof that we remain in him and he in us, that he has given us a share in his Spirit. God is love, and whoever remains in love remains in God and God in him (1 Jn 4:11–13, 16).

And so, the call is clear and the work before us is set out. What remains for us to do now is to act—to prayerfully act with clarity, courage, and a knowledge that we don't need to have special talents or achieve great things to have sound self-esteem, good friendship, or to find a way to God in daily life.

Instead, what is needed is the continued search to discover who we really are and who we are becoming in the eyes of our loving God. In other words, we need to recognize again and again in our prayer, scripture reading, self-reflection, and interactions with others that the spiritual life is not a rarefied form of thinking or mystical experience for the elite. Instead, it is simply an honest way of living. Our journey with God can be made much more simple if only we take the time and effort each day to remember that true ordinariness is indeed tangible holiness.

NOTES

1. James Fenhagen, *Invitation to Holiness*, San Francisco: Harper and Row, 1985, pp. 27–28.
2. Robert Coles, *A Radical Devotion*, Reading, MA: Addison-Wesley, 1987, p. xviii.
3. Norman Vincent Peale, *My Favorite Quotations*, San Francisco: HarperCollins, 1990, pp. 51–52.
4. Anthony de Mello, *One Minute Wisdom*, New York: Doubleday, 1986, p. 4.
5. Ibid., p. 15.
6. Thomas Merton, "Learning to Live," in *University on the Heights*, edited by W. Forest, New York: Doubleday, 1969, p. 7.
7. Henri J. M. Nouwen, *Genesee Diary*, New York: Doubleday, 1976, pp. 51–52.
8. Neil Richardson, *The Panorama of Luke*, London: Epworth Press, 1982, p. 31.
9. Quote attributed to W. S. Merwin.
10. Abraham Joshua Heschel, *God in Search of Man*, New York: Farrar, Straus, and Giroux, 1955.
11. John Winokur, *Zen to Go*, New York: Plume, 1990, p. 67.
12. Abraham Joshua Heschel, *The Insecurity of Freedom*, Philadelphia: The Jewish Publication Society of America, 1966, p. 59.
13. Henri J. M. Nouwen, op. cit., p. 84.
14. Thomas Merton, *Honorable Reader*, edited by Robert E. Daggy, New York: Crossroad, 1989, pp. 124–125.
15. *Peacemaking Day by Day*, Erie, PA: Pax Christi, 1985, p. 154; I am grateful to this wonderful publication for bringing so many poignant quotations to my attention; I highly recommend this "year of reflections" to you.
16. Thomas Merton, *The Wisdom of the Desert*, New York: New Directions, 1960, p. 6.
17. Ibid., pp. 22–23.
18. Peter Brown, "The Rise and Function of the Holy Man in Late Antiquity," *Journal of Roman Studies*, 61, 1971, pp. 80–101.
19. Thomas Merton, op. cit., p. 21.

20. Gail Marie Priestley, "Some Jungian Parallels to the Sayings of the Desert Fathers," *Cistercian Studies*, 11:2, 1976, pp. 115–116.

21. Anthony de Mello, *One Minute Wisdom*, New York: Doubleday, 1986, p. 78.

22. Kenneth Leech, *Experiencing God*, San Francisco: Harper & Row, 1985, pp. 139–140.

23. Yoshi Nomura, *Desert Wisdom*, New York: Doubleday, 1982, p. 14.

24. Henri J. M. Nouwen, *The Way of the Heart*, New York: Seabury, 1981, pp. 30, 79.

25. Henri J. M. Nouwen, *Genesee Diary*, New York: Doubleday, 1976, pp. 139–140.

26. Yoshi Nomura, op. cit., p. 83.

27. Anthony de Mello, op. cit., p. 52.

28. Anthony Bloom (Metropolitan Anthony of Sourozh), *Beginning to Pray*, Ramsey, NJ: Paulist Press, 1970, p.2.

29. John Berger, *Ways of Seeing*, New York: Penguin, 1977, pp. 146, 149.

30. Henri J. M. Nouwen, *Clowning in Rome*, New York: Doubleday, 1979, p. 26.

31. Yoshi Nomura, op. cit., pp. 28–29.

32. George Merrill and Robert J. Wicks, *Reflections*, Mahwah, NJ: Paulist Press, 1990, p. 81.

33. Thomas Merton, op. cit., p. 24.

34. Abraham Joshua Heschel, *Man Is Not Alone*, New York: Farrar, Straus, and Young, 1951, p. 179.

35. Yoshi Nomura, op. cit., p. 97.

36. Kenneth Leech, op. cit., p. 40.

37. Edmund Fuller, *Men in Modern Fiction*, pp. 163–164.

38. Linda Tschirhart Sandford and Mary Ellen Donavan, *Woman and Self-Esteem*, New York: Anchor/Doubleday, 1985, p. 7; this definition of self-esteem by William Appleton is quoted in this very helpful book on self-esteem.

39. Virginia Woolf, "Professions for Women" in *Virginia Woolf: Collected Essays, Vol. II*, London: Hogarth Press, 1966, pp. 284–289.

40. Michael Franz Basch, "Dynamic Psychotherapy and its Frustrations," in *Resistance*, edited by Paul Wachtel, New York: Plenum, 1982, p. 16; in this section Dr. Basch is discussing a view on maturation by H. Kohut.

41. Linda Tschirhart Sanford and Mary Ellen Donavan, op. cit., p. xv.
42. Caryl Rivers, Rosalind Barnett, and Grace Baruch, *Beyond Sugar and Spice: How Women Grow, Learn, and Thrive*, New York: Putnam, 1979.
43. I am grateful to Mary McCauley for bringing this quote to my attention.
44. I am grateful to Fr. Charles Crouse for sharing this information with me; the story was shared with him by Leo Rock, S.J.
45. This wonderful story was told by David Augus, burger of Fuller Theological Seminary at the 1991 Los Angeles Religious Education Congress.
46. Louis Evely, *That Man Is You*, translated by Edmond Bonn, Ramsey, NJ: Paulist Press, 1964, pp. 102–103.
47. Aaron T. Beck, *Cognitive Therapy and Emotional Disorders*, New York: Meridian, 1976; this classic is an introduction to his theory.
48. Robert J. Wicks, *Living Simply in an Anxious World*, Mahwah, NJ: Paulist Press, 1988, pp. 19–20.
49. A list of Albert Ellis' work is available through the Institute for Rational Emotive Therapy, 45 E. 65th St., New York, NY 10021.
50. For a more extensive treatment of this topic see: David Burns, *Feeling Good*, New York: New American Library, 1980; this is one of the best self-help books on the market.
51. Anthony de Mello, *One Minute Wisdom*, New York: Doubleday, 1986, p. 55.
52. "An Interview with Thich Nhat Hanh, Vietnamese Zen Master," *Common Boundary*, Nov/Dec, 1989, p. 16.
53. Arnold Lazarus, *In the Mind's Eye*, New York: Guilford, 1984, p. 36.
54. Matthew McKay and Patrick Fanning, *Self-Esteem*, Oakland, CA: New Harbinger Publications, 1987, pp. 172–173.
55. Arnold Lazarus, op. cit., p. 36; three audio tapes are also available from the same publisher under the title *Personal Enrichment Through Imagery*.
56. Anthony A. Hoekema, "The Christian Self-Image: A Reformed Perspective" in *Your Better Self*, edited by Craig W. Ellison, San Francisco: Harper & Row, 1983, p. 34.
57. Ibid., p. 36.

58. Ibid., p. 24.
59. Patrick McCloskey, *Naming Your God: The Search for Mature Images*, Notre Dame, IN: Ave Maria Press, 1991, p. 8.
60. Henri J. M. Nouwen, *Making All Things New*, San Francisco: Harper and Row, 1981, p. 33.
61. Source unknown; quoted in Pax Christi's *Peacemaking Day by Day*, op. cit., p. 61.
62. Robert J. Wicks, *Seeking Perspective*, Mahwah, NJ: Paulist Press, 1991, p. 36.
63. John Rogers and Pete Mc Williams, *You Can't Afford the Luxury of a Negative Thought*, Los Angeles: Prelude, 1989.
64. Abraham Joshua Heschel, *The Insecurity of Freedom*, Philadelphia: The Jewish Publication Society of America, 1966, pp. 164–165.
65. I have heard/read different versions of this story in a number of places. One version is contained in Isaias Powers' *Father Ike's Stories for Children*, Mystic, CT: Twenty-Third Publications, 1988, pp. 54–58.
66. Reuven P. Bulka, "Religion in Contemporary Times: For Denial or For Pleasure," *PIRI Newsletter*, 15, 1, Winter 1990, pp. 1–2, citing and commenting on the Jerusalem Talmud, Kiddushin, 4:1, New York: Otzar HaSefarim, 1968.
67. Yoshi Nomura, *Desert Wisdom*, New York: Doubleday, 1982, pp. 74–75.
68. This is a very loosely adapted version of a story told by Ronald Cranfields; I was first introduced to it by Marietta Culhane, O.S.F., and I am very grateful to her for having shared it with me.
69. Source unknown; quoted in Pax Christi's *Peacemaking Day by Day*, op. cit., p. 97.
70. Anonymous; I am grateful to Carmen Kozlowski for bringing this quote to my attention.
71. Quoted by the Dalai Lama in his very simple and enjoyable autobiography, *Freedom in Exile*, New York: HarperCollins, 1990, p. 225.
72. From *Tales of the Hasidim*, cited in *Peacemaking Day by Day*, op. cit., p. 102.
73. I am grateful to Fr. James Kelley for sharing this information with me.

74. Anthony de Mello, *One Minute Wisdom*, New York: Doubleday, 1986, p. 168.

75. Robert Coles, *Dorothy Day: A Radical Devotion*, Reading, MA: Addison-Wesley, 1987, p. 126.

76. When I was facilitating a clergy retreat in Alaska, Msgr. Francis Cowgill shared this story with me; I am grateful to him.

77. This is an adapted version of a story told by Fr. James Murphy, I am thankful to him for sharing it.

78. Anonymous.

79. Jeffrey Kottler, *On Being a Therapist*, San Francisco: Jossey-Bass, 1986, pp. 1, 8.

80. *Peacemaking Day by Day*, p. 134.

81. Anthony Hopkins, "The Lightning of Olivier," *New York Times*, Section IV, July 16, 1989, p. 23.

82. Matina Horner, "Introduction" in Robert Coles, *Dorothy Day: A Radical Devotion*, Reading, MA: Addison-Wesley, 1987, p. ix.

83. I am grateful to Fr. Kevin Egan for bringing this quote to my attention.

84. Abraham Joshua Heschel, *Who Is Man?* Stanford, CA: Stanford University Press, 1965, p. 96.

DR. ROBERT J. WICKS, who received his doctorate in Psychology from Hahnemann Medical College, is a professor at Loyola College in Maryland. He has taught in universities and professional schools of psychology, medicine, social work, nursing, and theology. His two major areas of expertise are the prevention of secondary stress (the pressures encountered in reaching out to others) and the integration of psychology and spirituality from a world religion perspective. He has addressed 10,000 educators in the Air Canada Arena in Toronto, spoken at the FBI Academy, led a weeklong course in Paris, and was commencement speaker at Stritch School of Medicine.

In 1994, he was responsible for the psychological debriefing of relief workers evacuated from Rwanda during their bloody civil war. In 1993, and again in 2001, he worked in Cambodia. During these visits, his work was with professionals from the English-speaking community who were present to help the Khmer people rebuild their nation following years of terror and torture. In 2006, he also delivered a presentation on self-care at the National Naval Medical Center in Bethesda Maryland to those health care professionals responsible for Iraqi war veterans evacuated to the U. S. with multiple amputations and severe head injuries.

Dr. Wicks has published over 40 books for both professionals and the general public. His most recent book for professionals, *Overcoming Secondary Stress in Medical and Nursing Practice*, was published by Oxford University Press.